New Frontiers in Education
A Rowman & Littlefield Education Series
Edited by Dr. Frederick M. Hess

This Rowman & Littlefield Education series provides educational leaders, entrepreneurs, and researchers the opportunity to offer insights that stretch the boundaries of thinking on education.

Educational entrepreneurs and leaders have too rarely shared their experiences and insights. Research has too often been characterized by impenetrable jargon. This series aims to foster volumes that can inform, educate, and inspire aspiring reformers and allow them to learn from the trials of some of today's most dynamic doers; provide researchers with a platform for explaining their work in language that allows policy makers and practitioners to take full advantage of its insights; and establish a launch pad for fresh ideas and hard-won experience.

Whether an author is a prominent leader in education, a researcher, or an entrepreneur, the key criterion for inclusion in *New Frontiers in Education* is a willingness to challenge conventional wisdom and pat answers.

The series editor, Frederick M. Hess, is the director of education policy studies at the American Enterprise Institute and can be reached at rhess@aei.org or (202) 828-6030.

Other titles in the series:

Social Entrepreneurship in Education: Private Ventures for the Public Good
by Michael R. Sandler

It's the Classroom, Stupid: A Plan to Save America's Schoolchildren
by Kalman R. Hettleman

Choosing Excellence in Public Schools: Where There's a Will, There's a Way
by David W. Hornbeck with Katherine Conner

p. 13
p. 14

Working for Kids

Educational Leadership as Inquiry and Invention

James H. Lytle

Rowman & Littlefield Education
A division of
ROWMAN & LITTLEFIELD PUBLISHERS, INC.
Lanham • New York • Toronto • Plymouth, UK

Published by Rowman & Littlefield Education
A division of Rowman & Littlefield Publishers, Inc.
A wholly owned subsidiary of The Rowman & Littlefield Publishing Group, Inc.
4501 Forbes Boulevard, Suite 200, Lanham, Maryland 20706
http://www.rowmaneducation.com

Estover Road, Plymouth PL6 7PY, United Kingdom

British Library Cataloguing in Publication Information Available

Library of Congress Cataloging-in-Publication Data
Lytle, James H., 1940-
  Working for kids : educational leadership as inquiry and invention / James
H. Lytle.
      p. cm. — (New frontiers in education)
  Includes bibliographical references.
  ISBN 978-1-60709-055-7 (cloth : alk. paper)— ISBN 978-1-60709-056-4 (pbk. :
alk. paper)— ISBN 978-1-60709-057-1 (electronic)
  1. School management and organization. 2. School principals. 3.
Educational leadership. I. Title.
  LB2805.L98 2010
  371.2—dc22   2009041869

∞™ The paper used in this publication meets the minimum requirements of
American National Standard for Information Sciences—Permanence of Paper
for Printed Library Materials, ANSI/NISO Z39.48-1992.

Printed in the United States of America

Contents

Acknowledgments

Over the course of my career, I have had the good fortune to study and work with many talented and dedicated individuals. I owe them a debt of gratitude for their role in my development as an educator and leader.

First, I am grateful to the students I have taught, the students I have served, and the students who have taught me. Their contribution must not be overlooked. And I thank my myriad school and district colleagues—the teachers, administrators, support staff, and secretaries who have made my career so fulfilling.

From my days at Stanford, I am grateful to the late Dean Thomas James, as well as professors Robert Koff and Frank Hawkinshire, who gave me a conceptual understanding of teaching.

In Philadelphia, I benefited greatly from the counsel of deputy superintendent Dave Horowitz (now deceased), who was my first mentor in the district, and superintendent Connie Clayton. From my first years in Trenton, I thank board president Abdul Malik Ali for his support.

At Wallace Funds, I am grateful to Mary Lee Fitzgerald, former education program officer; Richard Laine, current education program officer; and Chris DeVita, president, for their encouragement and support. I also thank Ira Harkavy and Cory Bowman of The Netter Center for Community Partnerships, at the University of Pennsylvania, who have supported my work during several intervals in my career.

At Penn's Graduate School of Education, I thank Susan Fuhrman, former dean (now president of Teachers College, Columbia University), and Stanton Wortham, associate dean, who encouraged me to become a practice professor.

Consultants and coaches Tom Gilmore, Pat Sanaghan, and David Green have had a great deal to do with any success I may have had and have been among my continuing mentors and teachers. I am grateful to them.

I thank Rick Hess at the American Enterprise Institute, who encouraged me to write this book; Juliet Squire at AEI for her assistance; and my editor, Lynne Frost, who did a wonderful job getting the manuscript ready for publication.

Without my family, my career—and this book—would not have been possible. Teaching is in my DNA. My grandmother, Frances Hickman Wilkins, began teaching in Niagara Falls, New York, in 1909 and later became a librarian. My mother, Mary Emily Wilkins Lytle, taught high school English in Buffalo, New York, for twenty-five years. My brother, Mark Lytle, is a professor; my sister, Fran Clay, is a former librarian. My older daughter, Sarah, is a middle school teacher, and my younger daughter, Jennifer, works in the education sector of the technology industry. One son-in-law, Joe Begonia, is a high school art teacher; the other, Jacob Cogan, is a law school professor. My wife, Susan Landy Lytle, has been a professor working with teachers for over thirty-five years, and before that was a high school English teacher. All of these individuals, over the course of my life, have been important influences and valuable partners in conversation about schools and teaching. My grandsons—Caleb, Eli, and Jonah Lytle Cogan—gave me one of my main reasons for writing this book: I hope it will help them understand what their grandfather did for a living.

Finally, I extend my deep gratitude to my wife, Susan. She is my muse, companion, and confidante—my lifelong love and support.

Preface

This is a book about leading for learning, and about how school leaders can create the conditions for learning for adults and children. It builds around my evolution as leader and teacher, and my own wrestling with the questions of how one learns to lead and how one learns to tie leadership to learning. I've also tried to address the emotional commitment, energy, sense of responsibility, and pressure that being an administrator requires, and the potential rewards that successful leadership generates.

STARTING OUT

My first teaching job (1963–1964) was at East High School in Buffalo, New York. Although I had no teacher training, I was a college graduate and the Buffalo public schools were desperate to fill classroom vacancies. When I went to apply for a teaching position, I was hired on the spot.

At East I was assigned three sections of ninth grade English, one of them an honors section, and two sections of tenth grade English, both for low-performing students. East's enrollment was almost entirely "Negro," the appellation of the time, because the school's boundaries had been gerrymandered to "protect" other high schools with white enrollments. The principal was an authoritarian former Army captain, white, whose disdain for the school's students was almost palpable. And I was the well-intentioned Ivy Leaguer who was going to bring enlightenment to my charges.

During the course of the year, all went reasonably well with the ninth graders, especially the honors students. They were the children of doctors, lawyers, and teachers who had no other options for high school. But the tenth graders were another matter. They were willing to come to class, but as to minding their teacher—forget it. They weren't violent or disruptive; they simply couldn't be bothered with the work I was asking them to do. I would go home after teaching, have a beer, fall asleep, get up at 7:00 or 8:00 p.m., and try to figure out what to do to survive the next day.

Although a few of my colleagues were supportive, I never became part of a team or department and never had much sense of the school as a whole. For me, the school was defined by my classroom and by a vague sense of how little concern there was for the students' long-term success. I knew we were doing a lousy job, but I didn't have a coherent conception of how the school functioned as an organization. Nor did I have any meaningful contact with my students, their parents, or the community beyond the school walls. My job was to teach the curriculum, give occasional tests and homework assignments, keep a record of attendance and performance in my roll book, and give grades in English every ten weeks.

I was painfully aware of my ineffectiveness and kept looking for the grail. The closest I came was buying sets of *Raisin in the Sun* and having my tenth graders read the play in class. (This was before the notions of Afrocentric curriculum had even been conceived.) Somehow the principal found out about what we were doing and was apoplectic. How could I possibly teach something like *Raisin*—no matter that the kids were finally engaged with something? He demanded that I get the books back from the students and immediately cease and desist.

THE OTHER END OF THE CONTINUUM

The following summer I got married and went off to Massachusetts to teach in a boarding school, an environment for which I was a comfortable cultural match, and my wife took a job teaching at a public high school in a nearby town.

My job was to teach five English classes, some of which met on Saturday mornings, coach soccer and hockey; live in a dormitory where I was the supervisor for a floor with thirty young men, eat seventeen of twenty-one meals per week in the dining hall where I sat at the head of a table with ten students in my charge; and attend Sunday chapel services at least twice each month. The job was a literal 24/7 for three eleven-week terms. In many ways it was fun and rewarding. My junior varsity soccer team had an 11-and-1 season. I was teaching academic English in what I thought were challenging ways. And I had good relationships with a wide range of students. The senior faculty were welcoming and supportive. I quickly became part of the community and got helpful mentoring and support from many directions. The school was enough like my high school and college experiences that it didn't take long for me to learn my way around.

There were, however, a few things that bothered me about the school. One was that varsity athletes whose behavior should have been punished for disciplinary infractions were given only slaps on the wrist while other students were suspended or dismissed for similar infractions. Another was that when the school failed to meet its admissions quota, it would admit students who didn't meet its standards. What concerned me was that these kids were offered no extra supports, and the school made no accommodation for their needs. Many of them flunked out at the end of their first year. In my view, what we were doing was immoral. But it didn't seem to bother the headmaster.

I solved the problem by leaving—and joining the Peace Corps. When I got to graduate school a few years later and began to learn more about organizations, equity, and socialization, I could see more clearly how insidious and exploitive the school had been. And I knew that I wanted to lead schools where *all* students were treated with respect.

OFF TO THE PHILIPPINES

Although I was enjoying my teaching and coaching, when the opportunity to join the Peace Corps came unexpectedly in January, 1965, my wife and I decided that if we didn't accept the invitation we were unlikely to ever do anything so adventurous and potentially so fulfilling in the future. So we accepted, resigned from our positions, and put our household in storage. Off we went.

Following training, we were assigned to Manila—the big city, not the barrio. I was just another American at the teacher's college—one in a long, long line—although I was cheap and willing to teach introductory courses at bizarre times, like Saturday night. It was a little like being back at East High School. I was in a culturally different setting, but my experience was mostly limited to my classroom. There was no orientation; it was simply assumed that I could teach the courses on my roster. The faculty was so overworked and so tired that there was almost no professional discourse; we never met as a faculty or department.

Meanwhile, my Peace Corps colleagues from Mankato State and other heartland places I had never heard of were off doing remarkable things—quickly learning local dialects, living in bamboo huts, and becoming valued members of their communities. My wife was having a wonderful experience at the high schools where she taught. Her colleagues invited us to their homes for family events, and her students were embracing her. I gradually realized that what mattered was whether you could do the job, not what credentials you were carting around (a lesson that made even more sense when I later became an administrator in Philadelphia).

ON TO GRADUATE SCHOOL

As our Peace Corps service was coming to a close, my wife and I decided that going to graduate school was a logical next step. For a combination of reasons we wound up at Stanford's School of Education, although I had only a marginal understanding of what would happen when I got there. But I knew that I wanted to give serious thought to working in urban schools. Maybe part of my motive was that I couldn't accept my failures at East High School. I had also had the chance to observe extreme poverty in the Philippines, and had come to understand how the United States' influence in the world was contingent on its ability to provide through example a commitment to eliminating poverty, racism, and social injustice.

I went to Stanford wanting to learn how to be the principal of an urban school that would make a demonstrable difference for its students. When I got there I found that the educational leadership program described in the catalogue was moribund, which meant that I had to design my own graduate experience. That was fine by me, and I jumped into everything that looked like it could be useful—organizational theory, group dynamics, teacher education, public policy, and research methods. For the first time in my academic career I found mentors—the dean, my dissertation chair, and other faculty members—who took me seriously, encouraged me, and pushed me. Although I was offered an opportunity by the dean to study education finance under his supervision, I chose to work in the teacher education program because I believed that understanding teaching, and being able to work with teachers, was key to improving schooling.

I became active in the graduate student governance group and was elected president in my third year. That gave me a chance to represent student interests with the faculty, an early experience in "managing up."

As I began to think about a dissertation topic, I realized that my emerging understanding of leadership applied directly to teachers in classrooms. I determined to study the leadership styles of beginning teachers, and how and whether those styles related to classroom management problems. (Now when I reread my dissertation, something I do about every fifteen years, I am amazed by the scientific lingo and amused by the extent to which it is autobiographical—a veiled attempt to understand why I had so much difficulty in my first year of teaching, and how I had styled myself as a teacher.)

DOING A RESIDENCY

While at Stanford I had learned about Philadelphia school superintendent Mark Shedd and the array of reforms he had generated in Philadelphia schools. I wanted to be part of a systemic effort like that. A friend's fiancée was Shedd's administrative assistant, and working through her I was able to persuade Shedd to offer me a position immediately after my graduation from Stanford.

Shortly after I arrived in Philadelphia in June 1970, I learned that Shedd was immersed in a bitter dispute with Mayor Frank Rizzo, centered around race, desegregation, and student protests. Recognizing that I was just another of the many white do-gooders who had come to Philadelphia, I declined Shedd's offer of a position as his administrative assistant and instead chose to work for the deputy superintendent, an old-timer and insider who controlled everything that went on in the schools.

I spent two years working for Dave Horowitz, and the experience was as close to a residency or apprenticeship as I could possibly have wanted. Initially Horowitz was uncertain about me—he hadn't had a vacancy in his office and I was a "gift" from Shedd. But as he watched me work and got a sense of me, his trust grew and he began to teach me about how the boiler room of a big-city district works. I learned money, personnel, curriculum, categorical programs, and, most importantly, central office politics and protocol.

My experiences in my previous jobs and my graduate school training had given me some sense of how to go about learning an organization. As an administrative assistant I took minutes at meetings, wrote proposals, and dealt with whatever needed doing. I also made it a point to visit the offices of the mid-level bureaucrats who controlled much of what happened in the district—teacher allocations and assignment, budget development, program planning, auditing—all the operations that make an organization function. Horowitz gave me leeway to work beyond my daily duties and responsibilities. And I wanted to understand what Philadelphia schools were like, especially the most challenging ones, so I decided to spend time in one.

I picked Gillespie Middle School in the beleaguered community of North Philadelphia, and asked the principal whether I could spend a morning a week there observing in classrooms and figuring out how to be useful. He was kind enough to accept my offer, and I quickly befriended the school's reading support teacher, an energetic and seasoned African American woman. I agreed to help her work with some of the school's new teachers, and she was willing to coach me on life in big city schools. She and I organized classroom management workshops, and we tried to help struggling new teachers survive. Gillespie gave me an opportunity to understand the day-to-day life and challenges of a struggling urban school.

As I learned the district culture, I began to realize that without field experience as a school administrator I would never be credible in the district. So I set out to get an appointment as a principal, a process controlled by regional superintendents who usually had long-standing commitments to protégés for whatever vacancies became available. By then I had learned that administrative appointments were usually made in sets of three: a Jew, an Italian American, an African American, and occasionally an Irish American. That appeased the ethnic professional organizations that controlled the promotion process through their alliances with various school board members, but I wasn't affiliated with any of these groups.

I interviewed for several principal positions in different parts of the city, with no success. Horowitz was supportive of my interest, but he made no effort to intervene on my behalf. Then the director's position became available at an alternative middle school. It had been started by Shedd and was now threatened with closure by the board as a cost-cutting move. None of the old guard was interested in the job because it looked like it would be terminated almost immediately, but I had little to lose. To Horowitz's amazement, and to mine, I was selected by the school's management team. In July 1972 I walked into the Pennsylvania Advancement School in the guts of North Philadelphia as its new head. I was where I wanted to be.

WHERE IT ALL LED

Over the next twenty-six years I would be a high school principal (twice); executive director for planning, research, and evaluation; a regional superintendent; an assistant superintendent in the central office (essentially the same position as my mentor, Dave Horowitz); and a candidate for superintendent. I would also be excommunicated for two years for refusing to do the (illicit) bidding of the chief of staff, and demoted from assistant superintendent to high school principal for refusing to sign a letter of resignation when a new superintendent was appointed in 1994. From 1998 to 2006, I served as superintendent of the Trenton, New Jersey, public schools during a period when the state was undertaking a wide-ranging, court-ordered urban school reform effort. But those are other stories, and they'll appear as the book unfolds.

Looking back, it now seems clear that I moved among extremes—from inner-city high school to elite boarding school, from first world to third world, from teacher to student again, then from student to administrator. I began this journey as someone who had spent the first twenty-three years of his life in a white middle- and upper-class world, and as someone for whom the constructs of race and class, equity and social justice, were at best at an "awareness" level. Graduate school gave me a set of analytic tools—group dynamics, organizational theory, school finance, socialization, cultural transmission, and research methodology—with which I could begin interpreting and analyzing the experiences I had had and the contexts in which I had lived and worked.

My "theory of practice" began to take shape from this accumulation of experiences and graduate study. With each subsequent job change, I used my previous experiences to guide me during entry and transition, and to help me determine what work needed to be done.

INFLUENCES ON MY THINKING ABOUT
LEARNING AND LEADERSHIP

The roots of my approach to educational leadership date back to my problems in my first years of teaching, followed by the deep experience in understanding classroom dynamics and instructional design afforded me while in graduate school. I was fortunate to work with Bob Koff and Frank Hawkinshire, both social psychologists and teacher educators who were doing cutting-edge development and research on teacher education, grounded in the premise that teaching requires leadership of work (i.e., class) groups.

In their view, when the classroom door closes, whether in kindergarten or twelfth grade, the teacher has responsibility for twenty to thirty students who need to be organized, managed, and led if learning is to occur. That requires a deep understanding of group and leadership dynamics, and that is what they taught me. Both Koff and Hawkinshire were also committed to inquiry as an instructional methodology—because they saw inquiry as a way to generate energy and commitment, and experiential learning as a way to deepen understanding.

My experience in working with them, and later in my career with Susan Lytle, Pat Sanaghan, David Green, and scores of wonderful teachers and administrators, deeply influenced my respect for the complexity of teaching, whether observing in classrooms, conducting a meeting with thirty-five principals, or teaching organizational theory to graduate students.

Peter Senge (1990) defines the key roles of leaders as designers, teachers, stewards, and generators and managers of tension. I would like to think that in each position I have held, I embodied these roles. As I learned the context, I acted as a teacher and steward. As I determined the work and began to move forward, I was attentive to designs that would help accomplish the purpose. As the changes moved forward, I provoked and managed the emergent tensions. And in every way possible, I saw my role as teaching and caring for the community.

Gareth Morgan's (1997) *Images of Organization* has had an important impact on my thinking as well. Morgan's premise, and the premise of this book, is that one's ability to act in or on organizations is facilitated by one's capacity to "read" them from different perspectives. Because most of us have spent most of our lives going to and working in schools, the challenge of seeing schools from new perspectives is particularly difficult.

Another important influence was my experience in "group therapy." While I was district superintendent in Trenton, New Jersey, we received a major grant from the Wallace Foundation to support leadership development. (We were one of only twelve urban districts across the country to receive the awards.) One of the conditions of the grant was that I join superintendents from the other grantee districts at the Kennedy School of Government at Harvard for a leadership seminar conducted by Ron Heifetz, author of *Leadership on the Line* (2002, coauthored with Marty Linsky) and *Leadership without Easy Answers* (1994). Heifetz is a psychiatrist who teaches and consults on leadership, and being in class with him is like going to a therapist. Members of the group presented personal cases from their work settings, and the cases became departure points for analysis and introspection. I wrote about the experience in an article in *The School Administrator*:

Certainly none of the participating superintendents anticipated that much of the adaptive work of our experience with Heifetz and colleagues would be personal. We expected to be challenged—this was Harvard after all—and we expected we might get help with the hot and thorny dilemmas of our school districts. But the emergent truth was unanticipated: The answer was within us. We had to act on what we were learning.

For me, this has meant dealing with people and situations I'd rather avoid; acknowledging my discomfort with conflict; recognizing my tendency to intellectualize and analyze rather than just do it; admitting that for all my espoused comfort with chaos and complexity, I still need to be in control (better to lead than to follow); and sensing when I am reverting to my comfort zone.

It's also publically acknowledging my own shortcomings and accepting that many of the things I've done in my six years in Trenton have made a real difference for the kids and the city. (Lytle, 2004, pp. 24–25)

LEADING INNOVATION AND ENTREPRENEURSHIP IN THE PUBLIC SECTOR—BY INCREASING CAPITAL

One of Rick Hess's challenges to me when he suggested that I write this book was to demonstrate how school leaders can be entrepreneurial in what appear to be conventional and traditional organizational settings. In trying to think about how my career has been illustrative of an entrepreneurial approach, I've found that English sociologist David Hargreaves's work on human, intellectual, social, and organizational capital has been particularly helpful. While acknowledging that financial capital and physical assets are relevant factors in school effectiveness, Hargreaves's primary attention is to intellectual, social, and organizational capital, which he defines thusly:

Intellectual Capital—the education and training of individuals.

Social Capital—the degree of trust that exists between the members and stakeholders; . . . and the extent and quality of the networks between its members and its external partners.

Organizational Capital—the knowledge and skill about how to change the school by making better use of its intellectual and social capital to produce high leverage strategies of teaching and learning. (Hargreaves, 2003a, pp. 4–6)

In Hargreaves's view, knowledge-intensive pursuits (such as education) require innovation to produce the "high leverage" needed to bring about transformational change. Hargreaves speaks further of "communities of practice" and "knowledge management strategy" as keys to innovation and transformation, and sees innovation as contingent on "the capacity of an educational system, network or organisation to mobilise its intellectual and social capital, especially in relation to teaching and learning, in ways that achieve high leverage, by a combination of incremental and radical innovation" (2003a, p. 6).

My attraction to Hargreaves's work stems from my long association with urban schools and school districts. Particularly in urban schools, I now understand that the key to helping students access the opportunity structure—college, work, military service—is increasing school and district capital by whatever means possible. For example, whenever corporate or university leaders have asked me how they could help, I have always responded, "Don't give us money. Give our kids access. Let them be interns or audit classes. Let them learn how organizations other than schools work." Getting urban students across these boundaries is the first step for both sides.

I would like to think that I have had an intuitive sense of Hargreaves's postulates over the course of my career, and that the successes I have had along the way can be explained by my ability as leader to develop or increase intellectual, social, and organizational capital in schools and districts. I have also been able to attract or locate capital of the more conventional kind—money and real estate—and to generate venture capital through reallocations and reductions of extant programs and services. For me, that has been the challenge and satisfaction of leading innovation and of being entrepreneurial.

WHAT FOLLOWS

In the chapters that follow, I have used a series of personal narratives, interspersed with commentary, to explain how my evolving "theory of practice" characterized my leadership and helped me fulfill the purposes I (and my colleagues and students) sought to accomplish. Each successive chapter reflects how my accumulating experience—tempered by reading, writing, and learning—deepened my understanding of how to lead in the new situations I encountered. My hope is that in chronicling my own evolution as a leader and my own learning, I can help others see ways to lead for learning.

My approach has been to use stories from my experience as a school leader to speak to the emotional commitment, energy, cost, sense of responsibility and pressure, satisfaction and despair, and opportunities to learn that characterize being an administrator. I interweave those accounts with references to the educational and organizational leadership literature, as I take on the promise of the book's title—to show how opportunities to teach and invent present themselves constantly: that as the school leader one is being observed during every moment of every day, and that even in the smallest actions one is communicating expectations and values, modeling ways of behaving and problem solving, teaching, and learning. At the same time, one must be aware of the "big picture"—the context, policies, community expectations, history, and all the other considerations that determine what needs to be done now and what will need to be done in the future.

The book loosely follows the steps in my career, from my first teaching job to my current position as practice professor. The first four chapters, Part I, describe my evolution as a school leader. Chapter 1 recounts my experiences as principal of three unusual Philadelphia schools: an elementary school, a middle school, and a high school. Chapter 2 deals with my promotion to the district's central office as director of research, evaluation, and planning, followed by an "opportunity" to take an unplanned "sabbatical" at the University of Pennsylvania.

Following my sabbatical, I returned to the school district as a regional superintendent and was subsequently promoted to assistant superintendent, events covered in chapter 3. A year after my promotion, ideological differences with a new superintendent provided another unanticipated "opportunity," this time to become principal of a troubled inner-city high school. That experience—turning around a problematic school—is described in chapter 4.

The next six chapters, Part II, follow my experience in Trenton, New Jersey, where I was superintendent for eight years. In telling the story of Trenton, I have tried to demonstrate how the leadership "theory of practice" I had developed over the preceding thirty years was tested as I led a demoralized and beleaguered district to a series of accomplishments that no one, including myself, had imagined possible. Trenton called on everything I had ever learned, and it required invention at very step. My experience in Trenton presses the questions of how one learns to be a superintendent, when one is ready to lead a district, how one determines where a district needs to go, and then how one leads toward that end.

In the final chapter, Part III, I try to make sense of all that has come before, addressing the questions, How does one learn to lead in ways that improve opportunities to learn? and How does one teach leadership to others?

I

EMERGENCE OF
A SCHOOL LEADER

I

Principal

Over the course of eleven years (1972–1983) I was principal of three highly unusual "alternative" schools, an elementary school and middle school (simultaneously) and a high school, each considered as a model and each attracting national and international interest. I was not the founding principal of any of the schools, but each taught me a great deal about instructional leadership and about student-centered schooling.

MY FIRST PRINCIPALSHIP

There was nothing ordinary about Pennsylvania Advancement School (PAS). It had been started as a demonstration school in North Carolina and moved to Philadelphia at the request of a reform-minded superintendent, Mark Shedd. Shedd's theory of reform might be described as instigating "dynamic tension," creating programs and schools that were so different from the conventional ones, and so successful, that they forced large-scale change through the example of their success. To support that mission, Shedd made sure that PAS received substantial alternative program funding from a stream of federal grants.

In addition to being a grade 5–8 middle school, PAS also had its own curriculum development team, a research director, and an outreach team that worked in other junior high schools, supporting their efforts to implement programs being developed at PAS. The school was divided into "houses," vertically organized groups of about one hundred students in grades 5–8, with a team of teachers, assistant teachers, and paraprofessionals who designed interdisciplinary, thematic curriculum units and provided all instruction.

The school was located on three floors of what had been a textile factory, covering almost a city block. When the architects designed the factory's conversion to a school facility, they incorporated "open space" ideas popular at the time. Each floor was completely carpeted, with moveable partitions dividing it into a few large open areas.

The students came from ten different neighborhood schools, either by parental choice or at the encouragement of their principals and counselors (i.e., many of them were considered undesirable in one way or another). In some respects, the school was an early example of a charter school because it had a great deal of autonomy. Although the immediate neighborhood had originally been a white ethnic community of mill workers, the mills had all closed and the whites were rapidly being replaced by Latinos from Puerto Rico and the Caribbean. The students were primarily African American.

The first director (or principal) of the school had been an independently wealthy educator and philanthropist who had paid for some of the school's staffing with his own funds. He had moved to another alternative school in Philadelphia, and his successor had been promoted to regional superintendent, thus creating the vacancy I filled.

So here I was—the new principal. I had had four years of teaching experience, only one in an urban school. I had been to graduate school. And I had spent two years as an administrative assistant in the central office. It wasn't exactly a strong résumé.

Getting Under Way

My entry to PAS was also unusual. During the summer of my arrival we were scheduled to host a large professional development program for teaching teams from the ten middle and junior high schools we worked with. We had a month to plan a two-week program for over one hundred teachers. But that turned out to be fortuitous. I had had lots of experience with group process training, and the focus of the summer was on team building. So I had an opportunity to work from my strength and to meet and collaborate with the PAS teacher leaders and administrators who made the school go. By the time school began in September, I had been able to learn a lot about the school and its cast of characters.

Dealing with the Unexpected

There was an unanticipated complication. The fifth and sixth floors of our building were occupied by another and completely independent school, the Intensive Learning Center (ILC). It too had been founded by Shedd, but in the case of the ILC the purpose had been to experiment with computer-based instruction and tightly planned reading and math curricula. The district's instructional technology department was also located on the fifth floor, and ILC served as its on-site development arm. (This was the early 1970s, and instructional technology was in its infancy.)

ILC was a K–6 school that, like PAS, drew its students from a number of schools in the area. It was also organized in houses of about ninety students, vertically grouped, with a teaching team for each house. For reasons that were never clear to me, the two schools did not like each other, and there was almost no contact between them.

In August, the ILC's director resigned to become superintendent in an upstate city. The central office, seeing an opportunity to save money, decided that it would make great sense to make me the head of both schools. Suddenly I was principal of two schools, one of them deeply resentful because they were being forced to accept as their leader the head of another school they didn't like.

Becoming the Leader

For me, one of the hardest things about becoming a principal (at age thirty-two) was directing people who were older than me. In high school I had had to stand next to my seat when a teacher entered the classroom, and I did not call my parents' friends by their first names. The senior secretary at ILC was my mother's age and had a son who was a university professor. Many of the faculty and the two assistant principals were older than me, one had a doctorate, and both considered themselves (rightly) as having more school leadership experience than I. And neither of the assistant principals felt I deserved the job.

The educational administration textbooks don't tell you how to cope with your uncertainty. As principal, you have the authority you need to control, direct, evaluate, reward, and punish everyone in the school. So it should be easy. But authority and leadership are not the same thing. And intuitively you know that if you have to stand on authority to justify your leadership position, you are not likely to succeed. That means taking a considered approach to becoming the leader, not assuming you are the leader.

I had a symbolic choice to make. I could locate my office at PAS, where I knew I would be comfortable, or at ILC, where I knew there would be tension. I decided that if there was any reasonable prospect of merging the two schools, I had better be in the more problematic location. Symbolism matters. I chose the sixth floor at ILC and set out to lead the two schools.

Learning the Schools and the Kids

I spent my early months observing the teachers at both schools, and watching how the teams and learning communities functioned. I listened as faculty and staff explained what they liked about the schools and why they felt we were effective. I was tutored by some of our in-house experts. At ILC, for example, the nurse was also a trained social worker and certified school counselor. She saw each child from a holistic perspective, which made a lasting impression on me. Whatever a child's presenting problem, the nurse always looked for more than the obvious explanation, and in so doing was able to provide assistance to children and their families that went way beyond the "duties and responsibilities" outlined in her job description.

The feature of the two schools that had the most profound impact on me was the strength and power of the team (or small learning community) organization. In every team, the personal connection between adults and children came before all else, and it made all else happen. Whatever the combination of team staffing—teachers, paraprofessionals, and assistant teachers—planning was always a collaborative effort with every voice respected and each adult important in meeting student needs. Teachers led every team and took great pride in their students' accomplishments. We were a "distributed leadership school" long before the concept became a buzzword.

Teachers at both schools planned team schedules, developed curriculum units, monitored student progress with portfolio assessments, contacted parents, and provided tutoring and small-group instruction as required. Report cards included extensive written feedback. There was no need for special education classes because every child could be accommodated within the team setting.

Early grade teachers at ILC regularly made home visits, organizing coffee klatches for parents living near each other. I went along and observed extraordinarily skilled faculty make parents comfortable and share techniques for teaching their children at home.

In many respects my job was to make sure two excellent schools kept on being excellent. That meant understanding and appreciating what we were doing, keeping everything on course, and recruiting highly qualified personnel on the rare occasions when we had vacancies. It also meant beating the drum for our good work.

Observing the Faculty

One of my long-time colleagues was a kindergarten teacher at ILC when I arrived as the new principal. She has often told audiences and me about what happened when I first did an observation of her classroom. All through student teaching and at ILC she had been considered a star—dynamic, student-focused, and exceptionally well prepared. Her classroom was considered a model.

In graduate school I had done a year-long ethnographic study of a first-grade classroom, so I had learned a lot about field notes, observation, and writing up observations. And that's how I approached observing Barbara. I wrote a four-page descriptive report of what the kids were doing, how the space was organized, and what roles she played. The report made no judgments about her teaching, but rather described her classroom from an outsider's perspective and posed a number of questions for her to think about and discuss with me if she wanted to.

By Barbara's account she was initially furious. No one had ever raised questions about her teaching before. But after she had taken a few days to cool off and think about the questions, she began to feel that they were worth thinking about. And she and I began a conversation about teaching and learning.

Where to Go?

It didn't take me long to figure out that both PAS and ILC were terrific schools—with hard-working and dedicated faculties; great support staff; all sorts of books, materials, and supplies; and a commitment to experimentation and accountability. In one illustration of the extent of their reputations, the Russian minister of education came to Philadelphia specifically to see the computerized instructional program at ILC. Both PAS and ILC consistently outperformed schools with comparable student populations.

But I also understood that both schools had significant liabilities. The first was the building. It had been worn out when it was converted to a school, and it wasn't really suited to its new use. Having kindergarten classrooms on the sixth floor of a building with two freight elevators and narrow fire towers was unconscionable. There was no gym and no outdoor play space, and the "cafeteria" was an improvised room on the first floor.

Both schools were closely identified with Mark Shedd, but the new mayor had driven Shedd out of town and the new school board and superintendent had no sympathy for alternative schools. The push now was for desegregation programs, and, because of their location, PAS and ILC weren't attractive candidates. In addition, neither school was a neighborhood school, so both were dependent on attracting students from feeder schools and bussing them, a cost the district was increasingly reluctant to bear. Both schools were heavily dependent on federal supplemental funding for alternative programs, and that policy initiative was shifting. Early in my third year, my contacts in the central office made it clear that the two schools were not sustainable in their current form. Our supplemental funding was going to be eliminated. Our days were numbered.

Rather than let the district determine our fate, we began to plan for combining the two schools and becoming a grade 6–8 middle school serving neighborhood children. Changing demographics indicated the need for such a school, and central office support for this new direction was relatively easily negotiated.

Merging the two schools and eliminating the lower-grade programs obviously didn't make everyone happy. However, we had announced the decision early enough in the spring that parents could begin making alternate plans for their children, and faculty and staff could determine whether they would have a place at the newly renamed Clemente School, or whether they would need to transfer to another school. Meeting with them to announce the decision was difficult for everyone. But most of the employees appreciated the candor and respect extended to them, and the adequate prior notice they had been given.

We completed the redesign of the school, supported the faculty and staff who would be transferred to other schools, and developed the feeder pattern for the new Clemente. Within three years, the two schools I had come to lead had been merged and their missions downscaled—partly at my instigation. A few years later the factory building was closed, and Clemente relocated to a new building designed specifically for it. The school had survived and become important to the community, but Shedd's dream for reforms modeled on PAS and ILC had evaporated. (In the years that followed, at least fifteen of the PAS and ILC faculty members went on to become successful principals, supervisors, superintendents, and entrepreneurs, suggesting that the schools' recruitment process and distributed leadership models had been factors in developing prospective educational leaders.)

Serendipity

I, too, was to experience a big change. Not all promotions are the result of careful career planning. I had been principal of PAS and ILC for almost three years when one spring weekend I took my daughters to a parade on the Parkway in downtown Philadelphia. By coincidence, I ran into my central office mentor of a few years back, Dave Horowitz. He mentioned that a high school principalship was about to open at the Parkway Program (named for the very Parkway we were standing on); he suggested that I apply. I followed his advice and a few months later was named principal of the school, an opportunity that provided a wonderful experience heading a leading-edge alternative program and that had a major impact on my later career. I sometimes wonder where I would be today if I hadn't gone to that parade.

MY SECOND PRINCIPALSHIP

For the next eight years I was principal of Parkway Program in Philadelphia, the nation's first "school without walls." Ironically, Parkway was another of the schools started by Mark Shedd in his efforts to drive reform by creating dramatic alternatives to conventional schools. Parkway emerged in the late 1960s and early 1970s as an alternative to conventional high schools. It used "found space" for classrooms—the YMCA, churches, museums, or neighborhood recreation centers—places that weren't fully utilized during the school day.

At its height, Parkway had 1,250 students in five different neighborhood sites (or units) scattered across central Philadelphia. Because Parkway teachers taught in the found space, students had to walk around the neighborhood as they went from class to class. The students also took many of their classes from volunteers at community-based organizations—hospitals, newspapers, and universities, wherever we could find good opportunities. It sounds a bit odd, but it worked. While attending Parkway, a cross-section of city kids developed aspirations and went on to college and work in numbers far exceeding those from schools with comparable demographics but more conventional approaches.

Parkway was the embodiment of a "loosely coupled" system, and it succeeded in part because it had a strong ethos (Lytle, 1980). But there had never been an "inspection" of how the teachers were doing their jobs because my predecessor principals had not observed the faculty. As the new principal, I decided that a fast way to learn the school was to follow the process I had used at PAS and ILC, and do an observation of every teacher. Given the school's geography, this was not an easy task. It took several months, and for each observation I wrote a detailed descriptive and analytic report, which I shared with the teacher.

The reaction of the faculty was consistent. Most said they had never been observed, including several who had been teaching at other schools before coming to Parkway. They were appreciative of the feedback and of the sense I was able to communicate regarding the complexities of teaching. Over the course of the observations I developed an overview of what the school looked and felt like, and what sort of education we were providing our students. I had a preliminary understanding of how to position our discussions on curriculum, teaching, and learning, and I was able to reflect back to the faculty a sense of who we were as a school.

Compulsory Entrepreneurship

Parkway was my tutorial in entrepreneurship. At PAS and ILC we had money and staff; the problem was to use them well. In contrast, Parkway was an intentionally under-resourced school. It had been created in part to deal with burgeoning high school enrollment. The Shedd administration decided that rather than invest in another high school behemoth, they could create a much more interesting school by using available, underutilized institutional space in Center City Philadelphia.

What that meant in practice is that as principal I learned more about real estate than I ever wanted to know. I was continually knocking on doors and asking whether this church or that YMCA would be willing to let us use a room or two for classroom space during the school day. The answer was often yes, but the organization wanted a small payment to defer costs. And they were worried about liability. That meant negotiating a lease, getting the district's facilities and law offices involved, and persuading the district to buy a blanket liability insurance policy that covered our students when they were out in the community attending classes, volunteering, or interning.

Because we were using the city as our campus, our students had to take public transportation during the school day, for example, going from a science class in West Philadelphia to a physical education class at Temple University in North Philadelphia. That required setting up a "free token" system to underwrite travel costs. We always needed furniture, and I became expert at renting a truck and raiding the school district's warehouse for surplus, or going to the Salvation Army, then having some of the students help with unloading. Another part of my job was to help maintain and grow a supply of volunteer mentors and teachers, ranging from a physics professor at the University of Pennsylvania to the editor of a neighborhood newspaper or the director of a childcare program connected to a church. In other words, I was as much development officer as I was principal.

Parkway was like an early version of a charter school in the sense that we had no neighborhood "feeder pattern"—which meant that we had to recruit our students. Selling parents on a school that had no building and that required their children to travel around the city during the school day was a challenge. We were successful because the school was safe—serious discipline incidents were unheard of. Part of our sales talk emphasized how going to a school without walls taught students time management and self-discipline. No one was going to chase you down the street to make you go to class. In that respect, Parkway was an excellent preparation for college. Besides, we were a good school with a good record. Our students were in many ways our best sales force.

But being an effective school wasn't necessarily sufficient. During one budget crisis the school board decided that an easy savings would be to shutter Parkway and send all the kids back to their neighborhood schools. We were able to make the case that Parkway deserved continuing support. Then I realized that the reason we were being targeted was because Parkway was displayed in the district's master budget as a separate program on its own page; that made the school autonomous, but at the cost of visibility. If the board needed to save money, all it had to do was tear out the page. The solution was simple—the next year we shifted Parkway into the district's senior high school program, which aggregated the budgets for all the comprehensive high schools in the city into a single display. Presto! We had become invisible.

I also developed a presentation on Parkway that demonstrated how low our per-pupil costs were in comparison to schools with big buildings. We had no security guards, no cafeteria, no library, no gym, minimal custodial staff, and a bare-bones teaching staff and administration. Yet in terms of attendance, dropout rates, college admissions, and test scores, our kids were doing markedly better than kids in schools with similar demographics.

Surviving Disruption

I had been at Parkway for three years when the district confronted a series of events that threatened our survival:

- Declining enrollment and an impending budget deficit caused the district to lay off more than 1,800 teachers at the end of June.

- The U.S. Office of Civil Rights determined that Philadelphia's school faculties had been intentionally segregated and ordered the district to balance faculties with proportional numbers of black and white teachers by school opening in September.
- The mayor was trying to amend the city charter so that he could seek a third term in office and needed the support of the teachers' union.
- The teachers' contract was set to expire on August 31.

After a brief strike, the teachers agreed to a two-year contract that guaranteed that all teachers who had been laid off could return on February 1, mid-year. The combination of layoffs and racial transfers meant that more than 3,500 teachers would be transferred before school opened, and 4,600 would be shifted in February. Of the fifty-eight teachers on the Parkway faculty in June, only thirty-eight remained by September, and for the fall term we were expected to teach the same number of students we had had the previous year with a faculty of forty-eight instead of fifty-eight. Not all of the "missing" Parkway teachers had been laid off; some of our black teachers had been transferred to other schools so that we would be "balanced."

The result was ten vacant teaching positions, but these could only be filled by high-seniority white teachers who were being involuntarily transferred from traditional high schools. These ten "new" teachers had never taught in an alternative school and had no idea what a school without walls was. They were given a half-day orientation on the first work day and were sent off to make their way.

The outcome became the subject of an article I published in *Phi Delta Kappan*, an educational leadership journal (Lytle, 1980). Within two weeks, the veteran white teacher transfers had been assimilated and it would have been hard for an unknowing observer to tell that things were any different than they had been before. The most important actors in helping these new Parkway teachers learn their way were our students. They taught the new faculty members how the school worked and helped them adjust.

When the mid-year time came for these teachers to return to their original schools, nine of the ten indicated that they would prefer to stay at Parkway. Every one of the Parkway teachers who had been laid off or transferred elsewhere wanted to return, although some were prevented from doing so by the racial balance provision. In all, thirty-eight of the thirty-nine teachers who had been caught up in the reassignment process wanted to be at Parkway. As one veteran teacher who had taught in the district for over thirty years (including five at a special school for the gifted) explained, he had never before had the opportunity to plan a curriculum that directly addressed the needs of his students. At Parkway, he found that both course planning and student course selection were reviewed by the unit staff as a group to make sure all students were given the help they needed. Another veteran said, "At Parkway I've been given the chance to try out some things I've always wanted to do."

These responses capture the essence of the teaching experience at Parkway, a school whose organizational design made it particularly possible for teachers to derive psychic rewards from their work (see Lortie, 1975). In my *Phi Delta Kappan* article (Lytle, 1980), I made the argument that the national and state policy emphasis on accountability, performance objectives, and achievement testing, combined with the increasing reliance on scripted curricula and classroom monitoring, neglected the motivational aspects of the work of teaching. I maintained that providing teachers with true opportunities to take initiative and gain satisfaction from their work was the key to our demonstrable success.

As to my own role in dealing with this turmoil, I think a big part of it was not panicking, and reminding everyone that we were a strong institution and would weather the storm. Another part was probably maintaining a clear sense of how the school worked and what its attributes were, especially what a good job we did for our students. And, finally, I provided a stabilizing influence by keeping in touch with and listening to those who were the victims of this mess, both the teachers we had lost and those who came to us as displaced veterans.

The Evidence

During my tenure, Parkway was selected as an exemplary school by the Pennsylvania Department of Education, cited by the U.S. Office of Education as an exemplary model for urban high schools, chosen by the National Urban Coalition as one of four outstanding urban high schools in the country, and designated as one of five truly effective high schools in the United States in a Department of Education study. This recognition reflected the fact that Parkway was demonstrably effective in improving the life chances of its students, as indicated by greater-than-would-be-predicted college, work, and military placement of graduates; high attendance rates; extensive community service activities; low dropout rates; low incidence of disciplinary problems; and high teacher job satisfaction.

One wonders why a school that was so demonstrably effective in teaching urban students didn't become a model for high school reform. We regularly had visitors from across the country and the world who wanted to see this remarkable school. We were even the subject of a television special in Japan. But almost no one went home and tried to do what we were doing, or even a part of it, perhaps because it was so different and unconventional.

Eating Crow

I also learned some important lessons at Parkway. Early in my principalship, I put myself in a box. The associate superintendent for field operations advised me that, because of budget problems, the central office was considering downsizing the school; that meant closing one of our sites, dropping teaching positions, and reducing enrollment. As a dutiful soldier I said I would get it done. I identified the site that in my view was most expendable, called a meeting with teachers and parents, and announced that this site had been designated for closing. Needless to say, the group was stunned and angry.

One of their questions was whether I had agreed to go along with this directive before giving them a chance to protest. I danced and dodged and finally had to admit that I had. Now they were angry with *me*—deservedly. I realized that if I was going to continue to lead this school, I was going to have to be an advocate for it rather than an intermediary between the school and central command. I apologized to the group and agreed to change my stance; I would advocate for continued funding for their site. The group mobilized and took their concerns to the teachers' union and school board, and we prevailed. The budget cut didn't happen. And I learned two important lessons: (1) don't equivocate—you'll get caught, and (2) stand up for your constituents—that's what they expect of you.

Back to the Central Office

As I was moving into my eighth year at Parkway, I recognized that I was spending increasing amounts of time engaged in community and district activities that didn't have direct benefit to the school. Although I felt I was making useful contributions in these activities, I also knew that I wasn't giving Parkway as much attention as I had in my first years there. I had been a principal for eleven years, three at PAS and ILC, and eight at Parkway. The signals said it was time to move on.

LEARNING TO LEAD

In many respects, my experiences as principal at PAS, ILC, and Parkway were grounded in the organizational and instructional approaches that characterized all three schools. Each was organized into small learning communities that gave teachers control over curriculum planning, scheduling, and instructional design. Because students stayed in the same community for at least three years, their teachers got to know them well, and the personal relationships between teacher and student created a kind of reciprocal obligation that made accountability a personal expectation, not an institutional one. All three schools used what would now be called "constructivist" approaches, with thematic units, integrated curriculum units, and hands-on learning. The teaching was engaging. And at Parkway, because much of the learning took place in the community, the experience of real-world work-study and internship opportunities was a powerful motivator for the students.

In observing how teachers worked together in small learning communities at each school and how these communities countered the isolation of teaching, I came to understand that professional collaboration was a key feature of effective schooling. In seeing how important secretaries and other support staff were in counseling and mentoring our students, and how creative our faculties could be, I learned about the importance of the tacit knowledge rooted in each employee's actions and experiences, and how we could be stronger to the degree we drew on this knowledge. And as I and the school leadership teams at the three schools tried to demonstrate the effectiveness of the schools to the central administration, I learned how to combine demographic, descriptive, cost, and performance data to demonstrate that our students were outperforming those at other schools.

Because much of the design and building work had been done before I became principal of the schools, I first had to develop a deep understanding of them before I could determine what leadership they required. In terms of my "theory of practice," I was principal in three schools that were relatively high-functioning when I was appointed to them—I didn't need to spend much time improving operations and could concentrate on growth and development. The faculties at all three schools were deeply committed to improving life chances for minority and poor children. I didn't need to bring a new vision or sense of purpose to any of the schools; I only needed to appreciate and reinforce what was already there.

Looking back, I don't think I became an effective school leader until my second principalship—at Parkway. Up to that point, I was still learning to lead. I was still managing rather than leading.

It wasn't until I went to Parkway that I came to understand how to lead for learning. In the instance of Parkway, that meant developing a clear understanding of the strengths and limitations of the school; encouraging risk, inquiry, and entrepreneurship on the part of the faculty; and supporting the faculty as the school developed its human, social, and organizational capital, and in doing so improving opportunities to learn for its students.

2

Central Office and "Sabbatical"

For six years, between 1983 and 1988, I was executive director for planning, research, and evaluation for the School District of Philadelphia and a member of the superintendent's cabinet. I was excited at the prospect of being part of a team that would restore professionalism to the district and, in the words of the new superintendent, ensure that "children come first." However, the process of being promoted was much more convoluted than I had anticipated.

In the years preceding my appointment, the district had been involved in a lengthy and dispiriting period of political intervention. Jobs and contracts were often the province of City Hall, and bitter teacher strikes were commonplace. Perhaps in response to that set of conditions, I had become increasingly involved in city and district politics during the years leading up to my promotion. To an unusual extent, determining how to position myself as the new leader of this large and complex office, while also following the lead of the superintendent, was dictated by political circumstances.

LEARNING (AND KNOWING) THE DISTRICT CONTEXT

During the mid-1970s, Philadelphia had an infamous mayor, former police chief Frank Rizzo, who deposed two superintendents, Mark Shedd and Matt Costanzo, for not doing his bidding. Their replacement was Mike Marcase, a former shop teacher and facilities division director, whom the mayor considered suitably compliant. Principals were dubious about having a leader who was so clearly a political appointee and sycophant. But things took a turn for the worse soon after Marcase's appointment, when a local newspaper discovered that he had been using district carpenters to make alterations on his vacation home at the Jersey shore.

Marcase claimed that he had intended to repay the district, and wrote a check for the estimated cost, but the damage was done. I remember attending a *mea culpa* meeting where he rambled on about the injustice of the accusations and asked for our support. But whatever measure of trust he might have had was dissipated. In a sense, Marcase knew the political context well, but he did not understand how important trust was to leading an organization. Although he was able to survive as superintendent while Rizzo was mayor by doing the mayor's bidding, principals paid Marcase's administration no mind and did what they felt needed doing at their schools—independent of him.

During this period I had gotten involved in city politics, violating an implicit norm that school administrators should not engage in partisan political activity. A neighborhood friend, a teacher in the school district, suggested that I become a Democratic "committeeman" in the ward we both lived in. That seemed like an interesting way to learn city politics and be a good citizen, so I volunteered and began attending ward meetings. That gave me an opportunity to meet and learn about candidates for public office ranging from city council to state legislature to congressional and gubernatorial aspirants.

The ward leader, Mercer Tate, felt he needed to concentrate on his law practice and decided that I would be a good replacement for him. With his support I unexpectedly found myself the ward leader, a role I had never imagined taking on. Now I was attending city committee meetings and fraternizing with the Democrat machine. This was a contentious time in city politics as Rizzo tried to amend the city charter so that he could serve more than two terms as mayor. I was among the group, many of whom were African American, who opposed Rizzo and were pressing for an African American candidate for mayor. Ultimately a white reform candidate, Bill Green, emerged; he won, and served from 1980 to 1984.

At the time, Philadelphia's school board was appointed by the mayor. The nine members of the board served six-year terms, with three members appointed every two years. That meant that the "Rizzo" board remained in control for the first two years of Green's term, and Marcase remained in place despite his lackluster job performance and his distance from City Hall.

WHY ME (FOR THIS JOB)?

Through all of this, I was principal of the Parkway Program, the youngest senior high school principal in the city. I had been an active member of the Senior High School Principals' Council, regularly volunteering for committees and drudge jobs. At one point I volunteered to write a position paper on discipline policies and procedures as an expression of the group's dissatisfaction with central office procedures and support. The council was extremely pleased with the report, unanimously endorsed it, forwarded it to the superintendent, and then pressed for a meeting with him to get the central office to address our concerns. The outcome was considered a victory, and as an unintended consequence led to my election as vice-chair of the council, and two years later, in 1981, to the chair position. Because at that time many of the informal leaders and seasoned administrators of the district were senior high school principals, being chair of the council gave me visibility, power, and access to the central office.

In 1982, Mayor Green gained control of the school board and his new appointees quickly arranged for the departure of superintendent Marcase. But the question of a successor was contentious. There were three prospective internal candidates: Dick Hanusey, white Ukrainian associate superintendent; Ed Forte, white Italian district superintendent; and Connie Clayton, African American female associate superintendent. Although all three were competent, in my view Clayton was the right candidate for the time. She was a consummate professional, had done a superlative job with early childhood programs, and would be the district's first African American superintendent, an important consideration given that two-thirds of the district's students were African American.

I contacted Clayton and offered to become part of her informal advisory group, which was in a sense a campaign team. Every few weeks I would stop by her office and we would talk about senior high schools, the district's major challenges, union politics, the city's circumstances, and whatever was on her mind. Given my experience as ward leader and Senior High School Principals' Council chair, she seemed pleased to have my counsel. And in my informal contacts with various city influentials, I chatted up her candidacy.

My sense and her sense was that the context for the superintendent selection was highly politicized, and that's how we discussed her prospects and "platform." In the fall of 1982, she was named superintendent and I assumed that I would be one of her early appointments to a senior administrative position.

GETTING THE JOB

But that was not how it worked out. Although Clayton made several direct appointments to her senior staff, I was not one of them. I was miffed. I thought I had done all the right things, including providing exemplary school leadership at Parkway, but that didn't seem to be sufficient. Several months went by before an advertisement appeared for the executive director of the Office of Planning, Research, and Evaluation. The job description was appealing, and given my research training and field experience, I thought I would make a good candidate. But the selection process was highly unusual for a cabinet-level position, requiring a civil service exam with written and oral components. I took the written exam along with at least twenty other candidates, earned a high score, and was invited for an interview. I emerged as the preferred candidate, much to the dismay of the office's testing director, who considered himself the obvious choice.

I was soon appointed, and in retrospect I understood that by conducting the process this way, Clayton had made the appointment as a "merit selection," thereby depoliticizing a position that had previously been a purely political one. (My predecessor as executive director of the office, Bernie Solomon, had been chair of the "Educators for Rizzo" campaign committee and had been rewarded for his service by being given a well-paid administrative appointment to a job for which he had no apparent qualifications.)

LEARNING THE OFFICE CONTEXT

Now I was in charge of an office with fifty-one professional employees, the majority of whom had doctorates. The office managed the district's student information system (database), evaluated all categorically funded programs (federal, state, and foundation grants), designed and coordinated the school planning process, conducted all testing and assessment programs, and took the lead in explaining district performance to the board and the public. In addition, as a member of the superintendent's cabinet, I was expected to participate in policy formulation regarding strategic planning and allocation of resources, and to consult with federal, state, municipal, and private agencies on proposed and ongoing categorically funded projects.

The office had professional (as opposed to politically connected) managers and worked reasonably well at an operational level, but it had deep morale problems because the district's mission had been so politicized and amorphous for almost a decade. Much of the work of the office was doing mandated evaluations for federal programs, as well as monitoring program participation. Because the audience for much of this work was state and federal bureaucrats, the contribution to informing school practice was minimal.

DETERMINING THE WORK

Role of central office

Because I had been a principal for the preceding eleven years, my orientation was toward designing the work of our office so that we would be seen as a resource by principals and school communities, and so that our work would contribute as directly as possible to theirs. To ensure that we had more contact and engagement with our "clients," we created "district research associate" positions based in the eight district offices rather than in the central office. The primary responsibility of these research associates was to work directly with the schools in their regions in planning and interpreting test and evaluation data. But they were also to be our "eyes and ears," acting as our scanning and sensing mechanism, helping our office shape its services and work in response to school needs.

As head of the office, my first priority had to be supporting the superintendent. I also had to stay attentive to all sides of the discourse—at cabinet meetings, in my conversations with principals, and in my interactions with the media—to get a sense of how the superintendent's agenda was being perceived and enacted. At another level, I needed to keep in mind that we were a child-serving organization, not simply 25,000 employees on the public payroll. As a principal that had been easy; the kids were there every day to remind me of their energy, interests, and concerns.

The challenge for our office was to be of as much help as possible to the new superintendent as she worked to restore the district's credibility and deal with a moribund instructional program. Her priorities included moving to a standardized curriculum for all district schools, and making schools the focus for accountability and improved organizational performance. In response, our office considered how we could best contribute to "systemic improvement."

BUILDING CAPACITY AND DOING THE WORK

In addition to our continuing operational responsibilities (e.g., maintaining the district's student database), our office launched a number of initiatives, including:

- Conceptualizing and implementing a school improvement planning model that involved teachers in significant ways.
- Developing and making widely accessible detailed annual performance profiles and demographic information for all 260 schools in the district. These profiles helped district staff, parents, and community organizations approach school improvement from a rich information base.
- Developing, in conjunction with CTB/McGraw-Hill and the district's curriculum division, a curriculum-referenced citywide testing program that provided national norm reports (the first new tests in fourteen years).
- Organizing a series of evaluation studies on the district's academic support programs, including Chapter I and special education for the mildly handicapped, leading to major reconceptualizations of these programs and integration of student support services.
- Providing technical support, scenario testing, and evaluation for the district's ongoing efforts to desegregate schools under state court supervision.
- With the help of the district's federal programs office and demographers at Temple University, designing a free and reduced-price lunch eligibility system that dramatically simplified the process for qualifying children, while increasing participation in the subsidized meals programs.
- Developing collaborative research relationships with a number of Philadelphia-area institutions, including Temple University, University of Pennsylvania, Bryn Mawr, Rutgers, and Research for Better Schools.

Example: Entrepreneurship in Test Invention

The test development project we undertook with CTB/McGraw-Hill illustrates how a district–corporate partnership could lead to an innovation in testing design that had direct benefit for the district and for CTB. Testing programs such as those provided by CTB had historically focused on norm-referenced reporting that allowed a district or school to compare its students' performance with that of students in other districts across the country. The problem was that these tests did not measure performance in relation to the district's curriculum.

The district was putting a great deal of effort into developing a standardized curriculum for all grades, and we wanted an assessment program that would determine whether students were learning the curriculum. But we also needed nationally normed tests for evaluating our federally funded programs, and for determining our progress in relation to our own baseline and other districts.

The solution sounds simple, but it was technically complex. Working with CTB, we designed tests that had enough items to generate national norm scores (e.g., 65 of 100) and enough items to determine whether students were learning our reading and language arts or math curricula (e.g., 60 of 100). The trick was to use some items that served both purposes and some that served one but not the other. The result was a new testing program that served our purposes and became a new product for CTB, with costs being shared.

Example: School Profiles

Our office was responsible for the *Superintendent's Management Information System,* a manual that was normally distributed to select members of the superintendent's cabinet. I was determined to make school-specific data readily available to the entire school district community. The solution was "school profiles," statistical descriptions of each school in the district, published in book format, that included everything from student demographics to teacher qualifications to test scores and promotion and retention data. The profiles had no evaluative component because I assumed that principals, teachers, and parents would be inclined to look at their own schools first, then at comparable schools, and draw their own conclusions. Our intent was to encourage transparency in school assessment.

Over time, additional data elements were incorporated into the profiles, and we began to distribute the school profile book each year to principals, public libraries, employee organizations, parent and community groups, and anyone who requested a copy. (Today, the document is published on the district's website and updated as data became available, with an archive for past years.) The purpose was to provide the entire school district community with the kind of information that would allow comparisons and promote inquiry. We did not assign values to any particular data element; that was left to the reader.

Example: Studying the District's Special Education Program

Some of the questions that emerged from these cross-school comparisons focused on apparent discrepancies in special education referral rates. Why would two similar elementary schools have drastically different referral rates? The temptation was for the central office to assume that the school with high referrals needed to address this "problem" and work to reduce referrals. But that would not be in keeping with Donaldson's (2001) counsel that we go beyond immediate solutions to a deeper critique of purpose and current practice.

That was why we decided to undertake a close study of special education referrals. Working in collaboration with the division of special education, our research team did a careful review of the records of a sample of mildly handicapped students across all grades. We knew that a disproportionate number of these students were African American boys. As we examined initial referral documents and psychological exams, we learned that the predominant reasons for referral were behavior in the early grades and reading problems that did not meet the standard for the student having special needs. Instead, special education classes were being used as a repository for those students whom teachers (and schools) didn't know how to help. That recognition led to rethinking support systems for students in early grades with an emphasis on prereferral assessment and early intervention.

BECOMING PART OF A NATIONAL NETWORK

I also became an active member of the research directors group of the Council of Great City Schools. Both the superintendent and board president were providing leadership for the council, pressing it to take an active role in lobbying Congress and advocating for urban districts. That meant that I was encouraged to organize or participate in research studies conducted by the research directors in the fifty member cities. Because those cities included New York, Los Angeles, Chicago, and Miami-Dade, we were collaborating with districts with influence and leverage on topics of mutual interest. That also meant that some of the work in our office was tied directly to national urban school research, providing strong motivation for our staff.

Among the projects we conducted were studies on dropout rates and on special education programs for mildly handicapped students. The latter study produced several compelling findings regarding the shortcomings of special education, for example, evidence that long-term special education placement led to *declines* in IQ scores and that there were no discernible benefits to being in special education classes. (I published a version of our report in *Harvard Educational Review* [Lytle, 1988].) The visibility and credibility of our collaboration with the Council contributed to our legitimacy as an office and our influence within the district.

Part of my leadership approach for the office was to encourage participation in national research organizations and conferences. We set aside a substantial travel budget, and provided support for every staff member who had a paper accepted at the American Educational Research Association Annual Meetings and similar professional meetings.

KEEPING IN TOUCH

As a central office bureaucrat I was concerned about keeping the reality of school close. I was all too aware of how easy it is to begin believing that what happens in the central office is more important than what happens in the schools. I felt I needed a constant reminder of the business we were in and of who our clients were. I chose an elementary school about a half mile from our office building and arranged with the principal and a third grade teacher to allow me to visit every week, acting as a "reading aide" in the teacher's classroom, a pattern I maintained for several years. My interactions with the students and my discussions with the teacher about her challenges kept me grounded, reminding me that all the "high talk" of the central office needed to be tempered by the daily "in-your-faceness" of the school.

SPOKESPERSON ON DISTRICT PERFORMANCE

Gradually, another of my roles became serving as spokesperson to the media regarding district plans and performance. The superintendent did not like dealing with the media but knew she needed credible representatives, and not just those in the public relations office. As head of planning, research, and evaluation, I obviously had access to much of the information the media wanted, and I developed good working relationships with a number of reporters. But I had to be careful not to overstep, and I had to anticipate how the superintendent might want a particular story presented so that it reflected her views and not mine.

My role became more complicated during my second year as executive director when the *Philadelphia Inquirer* did a series of profiles on the Clayton administration leadership team. I was characterized as "the keeper of the big picture," a description that was probably accurate in some measure but that also made me a touch uncomfortable. I had no doubt that the superintendent was the real keeper of the big picture, and I had no interest in being portrayed in a way that might suggest I was impressed with my own importance.

LEAVING BECAUSE . . .

I was viewed as doing an excellent job leading the office and got along well with the superintendent and most of my colleagues, but my relationship with the superintendent's chief of staff was cordial at best. One fall afternoon I was summoned to his office, directed to demote two senior administrators in our office, and sent on my way. No reason was given. My immediate reaction was anger. That night I wrote him a three-page letter refusing to do what he had ordered, arguing that his directive was unjust, untimely, unwarranted, and illegal. I delivered the letter the next morning. That afternoon I was again summoned to his office. He said, "Don't worry. I don't get mad. I just get even."

All went well for the next several months, and I assumed the matter had been forgotten. Then in late spring I was again summoned to the chief of staff's office and told that he had arranged for me to be assigned to the School of Education at the University of Pennsylvania as a "loaned executive" for the next two years. Two Penn professors were being loaned to the district to help with its desegregation and high school reform programs, and I was to be the counterpart. I was stunned and furious. What right did he, a relative newcomer in the district, have to meddle with my life and career? But I knew the deal had been done and that he must have had the superintendent's authorization, although I was virtually certain that he hadn't explained his true motives to her.

As I considered my fate over the next several days, I decided that things could be a lot worse. I was going to have the equivalent of a fully paid, two-year sabbatical. Recognizing that I actually had leverage because he wanted me out, I retained a lawyer who specialized in unlawful dismissals and had him draft an employment agreement that specified my right-of-return to the district in positions parallel to the one I was leaving. The agreement was signed, I was now protected, and off I went to be a professor for two years.

AN UNANTICIPATED SABBATICAL

My wife had been a graduate student and faculty member at Penn's Graduate School of Education, so I knew a good deal about the place and had met many of the faculty socially. The major professor in educational leadership had resigned to take a position elsewhere, so I was a welcome replacement. I quickly made myself useful and developed a teaching schedule, including courses in organizational theory, urban education, public policy, and research planning. The return to teaching—especially teaching undergraduate and graduate students—reminded me in a hurry of how much more carefully one reads when one has to teach.

Two things stand out from that period. The first emerged from teaching an undergraduate course in urban education. The undergraduates were smart, socially concerned, and mostly from privileged backgrounds. One of their assignments was to spend a day shadowing students in Philadelphia schools and to write an ethnographic description of the students' experiences. As someone who had spent many years in urban schools, I thought I had some sense of what student life was like. But many of the reports were horrifying, describing scenes and experiences that bordered on malpractice. I was powerfully reminded of how much work needed to be done if the city's disadvantaged kids were going to have any chance. (I still hear from students in that course who went on to careers in urban schooling.)

The other lasting impression came out of using Gareth Morgan's (1997) book *Images of Organization* as the primary text in my organizational theory course. His approach to using metaphor as a way to see and read organizations had a profound influence on me, giving me a new set of perspectives for making sense of schools in general, urban schools in particular, and urban school districts.

During this period I also had time to write about urban educational issues and about my view of large urban public school systems. I published articles in refereed journals (*Urban Education* and *The Urban Review*) and in professional magazines (*The School Administrator, Educational Leadership,* and *Education Week*), and I presented several papers at scholarly meetings (e.g., American Educational Research Association). I also kept a careful distance from the school district, appearing only on the rare occasions when my presence was requested.

In many respects, this unanticipated return to academia gave me the opportunity to "get on the balcony" (Heifetz & Linsky, 2002) and engage in reflective practice (Schon, 1983). After eighteen intense years as a principal and central office administrator, I could look back on the work I had done, think about how I might have done things better, and consider how I might approach whatever job I would take on my return to being a practitioner. I could also spend time thinking about social justice and equity issues, as well as effective pedagogies, programs, and schools. Not many educators get this sort of opportunity for renewal in mid-career, and I was fortunate to find myself in a situation that encouraged contemplative work.

As the end of my "loaned" period approached, I sent a letter to the superintendent advising her of my intent to return. During my absence, my nemesis, the chief of staff, had fallen into disfavor, and I was welcomed back, not as executive director for planning, research, and evaluation, but as a newly appointed regional superintendent, charged by the superintendent with redefining the role. The wheel had turned.

LEADING TO SUPPORT LEARNING

In one sense, becoming head of planning, research, and evaluation was like becoming principal of Pennsylvania Advancement School, the Intensive Learning Center, and Parkway. The staff was competent and highly professional, and things operated reasonably well. The difference here was that the staff was demoralized from having been poorly led and too directly affected by a dark period in the district's history.

My challenge this time was to rebuild a sense of purpose and efficacy—to remind the staff why they entered the education field in the first place. My assessment was that we needed to become less concerned with routine compliance and maintenance work (though it still had to be done, of course) and more concerned with how we could contribute to improving teaching and learning in schools. Over time, we were able to commit a good deal of our energy to designing and building products and services that enhanced our worth to the district and to those working in the schools.

My sabbatical at Penn provided me time to reflect, gain perspective, make sense of the work I had been doing, deepen my theoretical understanding, improve my teaching, and consider how to go about improving performance and opportunity in urban schools. When the superintendent asked me to return as a regional superintendent and redefine the job, I felt I was ready for the challenge.

3

Regional and
Assistant Superintendent

Almost overnight I moved from the sedate life of a university faculty member to the intense and demanding role of a senior administrator in a large and complex urban school system. I had been an elementary, middle school, and high school principal, but all those experiences had been in "alternative" schools that were considered outside the mainstream. And I had been a central office administrator, but not in a "line" position with direct responsibility for a group of schools. In my new position I would be supervising principals and their school faculties and staff, as well as a support staff, and I would be accountable for the performance of a group of schools whose enrollment was larger than most school districts in the state.

REGIONAL SUPERINTENDENT:
LEADING AN INQUIRY COMMUNITY

In August 1990 I was appointed superintendent of the northwest region, a subdistrict in Philadelphia, with responsibility for thirty elementary, middle, and special schools enrolling about 20,000 students. I was the region's fourth superintendent in five years. In the summer of 1991, a systemwide reorganization increased the region's size to thirty-six schools and 25,000 students.

"Regional superintendent" is a job unique to large school districts. Depending on how the district defines the duties and responsibilities of the position, the regional superintendent is the line officer overseeing all activities at all schools, ranging from school planning and budgeting to employee evaluation. But the regional superintendent is also a middle manager, the broker between the central office and the

schools, helping schools implement central office policies and directives, and helping schools get services from the maintenance division,
transportation, food services, and so on. During the time I served in
the position, our office had a support staff of fifty-five professionals,
including curriculum supervisors, a large special education support
staff, and administrative assistants. Almost all of these people had
been teachers, and some had been principals; they were a seasoned,
experienced, and a highly professional group.

As a regional superintendent, I did not have direct contact with
the Board of Education and did not attend board meetings. I and my
seven counterparts reported to a deputy superintendent and met
biweekly as members of the district's instructional council and the
superintendent's cabinet. My primary responsibility and that of our
office was to help schools do the best possible work they could, a wonderful challenge. My predecessor in the position, a long-time friend
and colleague, had been promoted to assistant superintendent for high
schools. He had left things in good shape—no messes for me to clean
up—so I had a great deal of latitude in deciding how to approach the
job. And the competence of the regional office staff meant that I could
use my time in ways that addressed system priorities.

The region itself was diverse. In half of the schools, 75 percent or
more of the students came from low-income families, almost all of
them African American; a quarter of the schools were desegregated
and had students from middle- and upper-middle-income families;
more than 90 percent of the students in the region were African
American, and more than three thousand were special needs students.
Of the thirty-six elementary and middle-school principals, twelve
were African American and seventeen were women; all but two were
experienced administrators.

As the new regional superintendent I was charged by the general
superintendent to "break the mold"—to demonstrate that the job
could be done in less conventional and more effective ways than it
was being done, in the superintendent's view, by my counterparts.
Given that challenge, I determined that participant research (what is
now called *practitioner inquiry*) might be a powerful way to encourage
principals, teachers, and support staff members to become a community in which we would think, learn, and work together.

I did not begin with a master plan. Instead, I let my role evolve as
I reviewed historical data and interacted with the principals, regional
support staff, and others in our part of the district. I started the inquiry
by conducting a personal survey of the thirty-six schools, then I designed a series of activities, each one building on the last, intended to

help us pursue our collective goal of better educating urban students. (For an extended account of this process, see Lytle, 1996.)

Focusing on Retention

In the weeks following my appointment, I reviewed school-by-school evaluation reports from the previous school year. I was nonplussed to find that more than 20 percent of students in grades 1 through 8 were being retained each year, and that retention rates in individual schools with similar demographics varied widely. I was well aware that retention in grade has no discernible academic benefits and greatly increases the probability of dropping out (see Artiles, Klinger, & Tate, 2006; David, 2008; Hong & Yu, 2007). I decided that a field research project focusing on retention was an immediate priority. Furthermore, the project had to communicate to principals, teachers, and parents that the high retention rate in certain schools was a shared problem.

The first phase of the project, conducted during September and October, involved visiting two schools each morning, four days a week, to develop first impressions. By the end of October I had visited more than eight hundred classrooms. I shared my impressions with principals and district support staff in early November, noting, for example, that calculators were rarely being used in math classes and that the "holiday curriculum" was rampant (i.e., spending a good part of the morning lesson on Columbus Day, Halloween, Veterans Day, Thanksgiving, Hanukah, Christmas, etc.).

From November through February I conducted a second round of visits, focusing on classrooms and subjects in which failure rates seemed inordinately high. I selected the grade at each school with the highest proportion of students who had received Ds and Fs in basic subjects at the end of the previous school year. I then followed one class from that grade, selected by the principal on the morning of my visit. My practice was to shadow the class wherever they went until lunchtime.

Generally, I observed classes in basic subjects—reading and language arts, mathematics, science, and social studies—and sometimes one "cocurricular" class such as art or music. During classes I took extensive field notes, focusing on students and on how they were experiencing each class and school generally. The observations were cross-sectional in the sense that I observed each group of students from the very beginning of their day at school. This permitted me to be aware of relational issues in the group as they played out through the day and to see how the students behaved and performed in different classrooms and subjects and with different teachers. In self-contained classrooms in the lower grades,

I generally observed the same teacher for two to three hours. In classes in the upper grades, I would observe four to six teachers in succession.

I knew from the outset that in conducting this study I was violating a set of implicit norms about what superintendents are supposed to do. I was spending lots of time observing in classrooms rather than concentrating on "administration." Although I wasn't evaluating principals or teachers in the process, I was bypassing principals by interpreting what was going on in classrooms in their schools without asking their opinions. This violation of expectations was intentional: I wanted principals (and teachers) to know that teaching and learning were my first priorities and should be theirs, as well. Further, I wanted to provoke inquiry, to cause principals to wonder about what I might be learning through these visits.

As this observation cycle evolved, it became increasingly clear that the utility of my project would ultimately depend on the degree to which I could identify issues and questions that would initiate discussions of teaching and learning among principals and teachers. Some of these issues, such as the district's promotion policy and grading guidelines, related to recent decisions by the school board; others related to research on teaching.

Taking the promotion policy as an example, the ostensible purpose of such policies is to retain students who haven't met the standards for a particular grade and require them to repeat the grade as the remedy. But schools rarely evaluate the efficacy of this "solution," either in terms of its effects on future student success or motivation. I felt it was important that we give considered attention to such policies and decisions, rather than assume their efficacy. That meant collectively reviewing published research on promotion and retention, evaluating how schools implemented the policy, and actually studying students in our school who had been retained. The basic idea was to use research as a way to inform our practice, and to make that approach a norm.

As I continued my school visits, I became increasingly conscious of the asymmetry of the process. As the district superintendent, I could enter teachers' classrooms without notice or consent—something no one else other than the principal had the authority to do. Although I assured the teachers whom I observed that I was not there to evaluate them, they still seemed to expect that I would (or should) provide them immediate reactions to what I had seen in their classrooms. But I routinely avoided providing any feedback. Instead, I indicated that I would send them a report on the project after I had completed the round of observations.

For each of the thirty-six shadow visits, I kept extended field notes on everything from classroom furniture arrangements, to student responses to instruction, to recess activities. What emerged was a set of impressions, organized in categories and by topics. These I shared with principals and other administrators, but I did not share this first version of my findings with the teachers I had observed, because it was critical of much of what I had seen, and I had not yet figured out how to share the data in ways that were respectful of the teachers.

In many respects, my observations were similar to those of John Goodlad (1984). A great deal of classroom activity was boring, repetitive, unengaging, and vapid. It seemed intended primarily to kill time. But I also heard a recurrent lament from the teachers: The children they were teaching were different, they said, from the ones they had taught five and ten years earlier; their emotional needs were so great that the teachers felt constantly torn between teaching the curriculum and tending to their students' problems.

To reduce the asymmetry of the observation process, I decided to conduct a series of discussions with the teachers whose classrooms I had visited. Each of the ninety teachers I had observed was invited to the district office on an afternoon after school to learn about the study and to share issues and perceptions about teaching. The meetings were organized in grade-level groups of sixteen to eighteen teachers; of those invited, two-thirds attended. At the outset of each meeting I spoke briefly about my purposes for conducting the study; then I invited dialogue on organizational issues and constraints that the teachers felt were preventing them from doing their jobs better. Although the teachers felt good about being heard by a senior administrator, I was aware that I was skirting the difficult issues posed by my observations.

Principals were also concerned about my impressions of their schools and of the classrooms I had visited. Again, I gave them very little immediate feedback and restricted my comments to generalizations at district staff meetings, where I discussed major themes or issues the observations were raising for me—while acknowledging that I was still in the process of making sense of all I was seeing. However, I did distribute summaries of the sessions with teachers at a principals' meeting in mid-April, being careful to present them without attributing fault or blame. The ensuing discussions led to a shared recognition that, if we were going to provide more engaging schooling, we were going to have to talk more about today's children and how we could design organizations, pedagogy, programs, and curricula that were responsive to them, while addressing the district's instructional standards.

Learning about Our Clients: Who Are These Kids?

Having spent my first year on a "public" study of the region's classrooms, I decided to begin the next school year by proposing to principals that they conduct a student study as a way of deepening our shared under-standing of why students behave and perform as they do. Although we had been engaged in a variety of small group activities and professional reading the previous year, and my sense was that I had been accepted by the group as a competent leader, I was still anxious about whether the principals would be willing to undertake a project that was a radical departure from the usual regional meeting format.

I asked each of the thirty-six principals, as well as nine regional office administrators, to pick a single student to study intensively over a four-month period. The purpose of the study was to address three major issues the principals had identified as topics to work on during the year: alternative assessment, group leadership that supports shared decision making, and the urban child of the 1990s. The administrators were organized into nine heterogeneously grouped study teams of five members apiece. Each team met biweekly to plan the next stage of the project, share experiences about research already conducted, and prepare reports for the whole group.

The teams were expected to ensure that the students they selected to study would vary in terms of grade level, performance history, and placement in special programs. They were also asked to consider how they would inform the child's parents and teachers of the project. The teams planned the studies so that the administrators would gain personal knowledge of the students before they undertook the "insti-tutional" components of the project. Each step of the study was intro-duced at a staff meeting, along with appropriate readings, planning, and training; the "researchers" then had two weeks to complete that phase. After each phase, the teams met to discuss their findings. The sequence of activities was as follows:

1. Shadow the student for a whole day (or two half days), keeping detailed notes about what the student does. Write a summary of the observation, including key anecdotes.
2. Interview the student, perhaps taping the session. Transcribe the student's responses.
3. Interview the student's parent or guardian (by telephone or dur-ing a home visit). Transcribe key responses.
4. Review the student's official records and all of his or her avail-able work samples for the year. What does the "paper record" tell about the student? (The student's teachers might be advised early on to begin collecting work samples.)
5. Interview the student's teachers.
6. Keep a journal during the course of the study and record reac-tions to the process (including staff meetings), any incidental

information acquired about the student (e.g., saw her jumping rope in yard with three older girls), comments about the functioning of the study team and of the whole group, and anything else that seems pertinent.

7. Write a study team report that summarizes collective observations, the implications of the study, and the questions that the project has generated. This report will be shared with the whole group.

When the studies were complete, the regional office convened a research conference at which the nine groups presented their findings on the forty-five students and discussed the experience of doing the project. As we listened to the reports and considered their implications, a number of interesting conclusions emerged:

- All the principals agreed that the official records of their students were very poor representations of the children they had come to know.
- Several principals had chosen to study students who had been retained in grade; they concluded that there was no discernible reason why the students they observed should not be in their age-appropriate grades.
- One principal studied an "invisible" child, the sort who goes through school unnoticed; he found the child to be both complex and an astute critic of his school experiences.
- A middle-school principal could not understand why students in her school behaved as well as they did when so many of their classes were so boring.

More significant than these particular observations was an emerging sense among the administrator-researchers that they and their faculties could be critical of schooling in collegial and constructive ways. We had begun to build a learning community in the best sense, one where there was respect and appreciation for everyone's contributions and questions.

Focus Group Studies of Report Card Grades

In reviewing 1991–1992 report cards for schools in the region, I noted that schools varied widely in terms of the proportion of students receiving As and Bs versus Ds and Fs in major subjects. Moreover, this variation seemed to be independent of socioeconomic characteristics or grade structure (K–5 or K–8). To better understand the variation, I convened four focus groups of principals in mid-September and early October 1992 to discuss the 1991–1992 final report card grades.

Because focus groups work best when the participants are relatively homogeneous, the groups were stratified by grade level and proportion of As and Bs or Ds and Fs. Two groups included principals from schools with disproportionately high As and Bs, and two groups represented schools with disproportionately high Ds and Fs. The discussions were designed to be nonevaluative. A regional office administrator and I alternated as facilitator and recorder for each session. Principals were provided summary sheets of report card data, which included information regarding their own schools, the other schools in the group, and citywide averages. The facilitator began the discussion by asking the group to interpret the data. When the discussion concluded (usually after fifty to ninety minutes), the recorder shared observations with the participants. A group discussion of what we had observed followed.

In two cases, the focus groups were held during a regional staff meeting using a "fishbowl" design (in which participants sit in a small circle surrounded by observers). Written summaries of the four sessions were shared with all participants; no editorial or evaluative comments were added. However, the observations were reorganized into categories derived from the transcripts. (Principals commented that focus groups could be used with their faculties as a way to discuss grade-by-grade performance.)

One recurrent theme in these discussions was the perception that many teachers use grades as a control mechanism. Another was that teachers consider grades to be their private property, and they deeply resent any intrusion into their student evaluations. In schools with a pattern of high grades, there appeared to be a stronger sense of communal responsibility for student performance.

Principals Study Principals

For almost two years the school district had been heavily promoting shared governance and site-based management, and principals were becoming increasingly concerned about the changing nature of their jobs. During the fall 1992 term, the thirty-six principals in the region agreed to study themselves as a way of better understanding the role of the principal. They were organized in pairs, and each spent a day doing an ethnography of the other. They were also provided excerpts from *Principals in Action: The Reality of Managing Schools*, an ethnographic study of Chicago principals done by Van Cleve Morris and his associates (1984). When the field studies were completed, the participants were organized into data-analysis teams to share their findings and develop descriptions of their work.

Although researchers have regularly noted how isolated teachers are from one another and how unexamined and uninspected their work is, principals are even more isolated. It is virtually unheard of for an experienced principal to spend a day visiting another principal. So it was not surprising that the key findings of the principals' ethnographies dealt with their shared problems and solutions. The group's willingness to undertake a research project that violated the norms of the urban principalship suggests that they were beginning to accept and internalize the notion of practitioner research.

Teachers Train Principals

Because principals had indicated a concern that their knowledge of curriculum development in the basic subject areas was dated, the region devoted five staff meetings to learning about (1) the new standards issued by the National Council of Teachers of Mathematics, (2) whole language concepts, (3) new instructional technologies, (4) new social studies approaches, and (5) hands-on science. However, rather than bring in curriculum specialists from the central office or local universities to conduct these sessions, teacher experts from schools in the region were asked to design and conduct them—and to model the new developments and assessment methods in their presentations. At least one principal initially took umbrage at having to sit through workshops conducted by teachers, but the sessions were intellectually rigorous, highly engaging, and fun. Most participants responded very favorably to them. We hoped that, by acknowledging and taking advantage of the expertise of teachers in the region, we were continuing to develop a learning community—and distribute leadership.

A Seminar on Race and Education in Urban America

During the summer of 1992, a colleague and I organized a seminar for teachers, principals, and parents that was designed to explore the ways in which race affects the work of the school district and the life experience of students. Because discussion of race among teachers and administrators is normally taboo, even in urban districts, this was also an experiment to see whether a group of employees could talk constructively about the topic. An extensive syllabus incorporated current literature and addressed such related issues as discontinuity between students and schools, living in the inner city, demographics and the urban condition, and culturally appropriate schooling.

The seminar met for eight days, six hours per day, over a two-week period. The meetings employed a wide variety of group process techniques designed to help members of the group draw on their personal and professional experiences in responding to provocative material. For the twenty-five participants, the seminar was a deeply emotional, revealing, and informative experience. At its conclusion, the group resolved to assume leadership of the seminar, to continue working on the issues, and to think about how the entire organization might deal with them. Seminar participants shared their experiences with their colleagues during a staff meeting early in the new school year.

Redirecting Special Education

Because of my long-standing concern about the efficacy of special education, during my second year as regional superintendent I initiated a series of meetings with special education staff members (one administrator, six supervisors, and fifteen psychologists) to explore our differing perceptions of how students with special needs were being served by the programs in which they had been placed. So that we could develop critical perspectives on the programs we were managing or supervising, we read and discussed material that focused on such local and national special education issues as:

- The virtual permanence of special education placement, despite federal and state policy calling for mainstreaming and returning students to regular education
- The disproportionate numbers of African American and Hispanic students placed in special programs
- The connection between special education placement and the likelihood that students will drop out of school
- The evidence that students' IQ scores decline in relation to the length of their special education placement
- The scant evidence that participation in programs for "mildly" handicapped students has benefit
- The dramatic strides made in improving programs for low-incidence handicaps (e.g., visually impaired, severely impaired)
- The significantly higher per-pupil costs for special education students
- The generally high cost of administrative overhead in our district (see Lytle, 1988)

Needless to say, for a group of professionals whose careers have been dedicated to special needs students, these were not easy issues to confront. As an outgrowth of our discussions, we decided to conduct an in-depth study of special education programs in the region. By consensus, the focal question for the study was to be, "What's special about special education?"

From October through early April, we observed in classrooms and talked with representatives of school staffs at the thirty-six elementary and middle schools in the region, as well as at three comprehensive high schools. I visited a school for half a day with the supervisor and psychologist responsible for a particular school to observe in special education (and sometimes regular) classrooms. Generally, we observed in classrooms designated by the principal, the counselor, and the special education staff; occasionally, one or more of these individuals would accompany us on our classroom visits. We spent from thirty minutes to two hours in each classroom. The observations themselves were loosely ethnographic; no checklist or form was used. We observed more than three hundred classes. Following the observations, we would meet with the principal and with interested members of the school staff, often for lunch, and discuss the purposes of the study and their perceptions and concerns regarding special education.

From these observations and discussions emerged an evolving synthesis of the characteristics of special education programs and of related organizational and instructional issues. This synthesis was incorporated into a document that was shared with teachers and principals at each school we visited, and then revised as a result of our discussions. The process was intended to make the study as open and collaborative as possible and to improve on the shadow study of the previous year by including as many staff members as possible in the "meaning making."

Over the course of the year, those of us conducting the study had come to agree that, except in the classrooms of students with low-incidence handicaps, there was little if any difference in the pedagogies being employed by special education teachers and regular education teachers. Despite the fact that many of the special needs students had been referred in early grades for reading problems, neither the materials nor the methods being used in special education classes differed from those in regular education classes. Nor did we see more calculators or other assistive devices in special education math classes than in regular classes.

In June we met to address the question, "How can special education contribute to the accomplishment of the school district's instructional goals?" We reviewed the results of the year-long "What's special?" study and engaged in a series of planning activities dealing both with school programs and with regional office services. These discussions led to a shared conclusion that regional office support services needed to be reorganized.

Regional Staff Team Building

As an outgrowth of the special education study and related activities, the members of the regional office staff began to recognize that our ways of working were too bounded by our formal job definitions. The regional office had fifty-five professional employees, including sixteen psychologists, six special education supervisors, eight attendance workers, eight support teachers, four parent trainers, a nursing supervisor, a researcher, four curriculum and instruction supervisors, and other administrators. The staffing design for the office had been determined by a series of central office decisions over a period of many years; as a consequence the regional office organization was not based on needs identified by the schools in the region.

Early in my third year, the entire regional office staff met to consider how we might begin to rethink the ways we worked with schools. A volunteer planning committee, which included representatives from the various job categories, agreed to assume responsibility for redesigning both the organization of the office and the individual roles and responsibilities of the staff members. Although a budget crisis led to a 25 percent staffing reduction, the regional office staff began the next school year organized into service teams, each responsible for working with clusters of schools.

Budget Crisis as Opportunity to Learn

During my tenure as regional superintendent, a budget crisis provided a test of whether the inquiry-based approach I had taken to building a learning-to-learn organization in our region could be extended to the hard business of financial management. Shortfalls in city revenue collections and an unanticipated reduction in state subsidies meant that the school district faced a $60 million deficit that had to be addressed within a ten-week time frame. In addition, a federal decision to allocate Chapter I funds using 1990 rather than 1980 census data meant an additional $30 million reduction in the district's Chapter I allocation. Historically, the district had addressed these situations by making a series of centrally determined cuts (e.g., eliminating all art teachers), but the district had committed itself to site-based management. If that commitment was going to be real, then schools needed to be given control of the reduction process. Because the bulk of the district's resources were allocated to personnel costs at individual schools, the impact of the reductions would fall most heavily on school staffing. With decisions being made at the school leadership level, implementing budget cuts meant eliminating the jobs of one's own colleagues.

With the help of the district's finance office, our regional office designed a set of simulations to give principals, union representatives, and parent association leaders practice in making budget cuts that would have minimal direct effect on instructional programs. The simulations were based on fictional schools with challenges and resources similar to the schools in our region. By starting out with the simulations, the leadership teams were able to consider options that would have been much more difficult to entertain if they had begun by focusing on the real world—the positions of their own colleagues and their own school's programs. (See De Geus, 1988, for a corporate model of using simulations to facilitate organizational learning.)

The leadership teams were then encouraged to involve their school communities in setting priorities and reducing costs. In this way, the regional office was able to help schools make nearly $10 million worth of reductions without a single grievance filed or complaint lodged with the Board of Education. Many of the schools were able to use the process to make reductions beyond their targets, then reinvest these resources in high-priority programs. The process we had developed provided opportunities for participatory decision making and reallocation of resources and, importantly, provided a powerful model for leadership as teaching and collaborative problem solving. The approach was quickly emulated across the district.

DID ALL THIS ACTIVITY MAKE A DIFFERENCE?

Of course, the overarching question for any attempt to reorganize, reform, restructure, and try new leadership approaches is, "Does this lead to improved school performance?" During the three-year period from 1990 to 1993, the proportion of students who were retained (grades 1 through 8) was reduced from 22 percent to less than 8 percent; report card grades at all levels and in all subjects improved, both in terms of reduced failures and increased proportions of As and Bs; suspensions and requests for disciplinary transfers dropped markedly; the number of students referred for and placed in special education classes dropped substantially; and the proportion of special needs students included in regular classes increased significantly.

All Chapter I schools met their three-year school improvement goals, and a number of schools took steps toward becoming site-managed and site-governed. In many schools, teachers conducted research projects similar to the student shadow study because their curiosity had been piqued by seeing their principals do so. Although it would be inappropriate to claim a causal relationship between the administrative development activities of the regional office and student performance, discernible changes did occur during the three-year period.

DESIGNING THE SUPERINTENDENT'S CABINET MEETINGS

At the end of my second year as regional superintendent, Superintendent Clayton surprised her cabinet by stating that she wanted to turn over the responsibility for planning and conducting our meetings to any of us who were interested in taking on this responsibility. As someone who had been doing a lot of experimenting with meeting design and learning communities (and who may have complained covertly about how stilted our cabinet meetings were), I quickly volunteered. For the cabinet's annual retreat that summer, and for each of the meetings during the next school year, our small group planned the agenda and activities. The reaction from everyone was positive. Our meetings quickly became more engaging and more fun, and made better use of the talents and experience of everyone in the group.

Part of the superintendent's motive in challenging us to take on leadership of the cabinet was that several of the most senior and highest ranking members of the group were planning to retire at the end of the school year, and she was clearly staging the transition.

PROMOTED

On the superintendent's recommendation, I was promoted in June 1993 to assistant superintendent in charge of seven regions and all elementary and middle schools, more than two hundred schools. My work as regional superintendent had earned accolades from my peers and from the superintendent. But neither I nor any of us in the cabinet had anticipated that the superintendent herself intended to retire. In July, one month after my promotion, she announced that she was leaving, effective immediately. Although she offered no public explanation beyond the predictable "an appropriate time for my departure," those of us in the cabinet surmised that she was fed up with increasingly contentious board politics.

The ensuing year was in many ways a nightmare, as senior administration and an interim superintendent struggled to keep the district afloat while a meddlesome board president used his position to establish himself as a prospective candidate for mayor. Although I was able to make some useful contributions (e.g., helping the board prepare for the next teacher contract negotiations), in the main we were consumed by palace politics as various insiders maneuvered for influence and the board president usurped the role of the interim superintendent.

AND DEMOTED

That spring I was among the five finalists for the superintendency, the only internal candidate. I knew in some ways I was out of my league. In terms of the school district itself, I was reasonably confident I could provide good leadership. But I also knew enough about city and state politics to understand that there were lots of sharks out there, and I wasn't a good shark fighter. I decided to go through the interview process because I wanted to say some things to the board about where I thought the district needed to go.

With strong support from the city's advocacy community and the media, the board chose David Hornbeck, who had been secretary of education in Maryland and a consultant to the state of Kentucky as it designed its educational reform program. (But Hornbeck had never been a teacher, principal, or superintendent.)

He arrived in July, and among his coterie of advisors was the same chief of staff with whom I had had a run-in six years earlier, he who had engineered my "exile" to the University of Pennsylvania. My office was on the sixth floor of the administration building, the superintendent's on the second floor. For five weeks I got not a single phone call or memo from the new superintendent, nor was I asked to any meetings. Then in late August he conducted his first cabinet meeting. He distributed a letter of resignation to all twenty-five cabinet members and directed us to have signed copies in his office by the next morning. He would decide which to accept.

I was reasonably certain that I was one of his targets. I had been a candidate for the superintendent position, and as a white male I would be part of an all-white top management team. If Hornbeck had had the grace to meet with me and discuss my options, I would have understood. (The closer one gets to the top, the more tenuous one's position.) But he had had no communication with me at all. So I refused to sign the letter, and I was the only one in the cabinet to do so. That night he called me at home to ask why I had not submitted my letter. I asked what would happen if I did. He refused to answer. The next day I was told that I had twenty-four hours to pack up my office, and that I was being demoted to my last tenured position—senior high school principal. Some of my colleagues praised me for my courage; others kept a careful distance.

Six months later I was assigned to University City High School, a story I'll tell in the next chapter. (When I later applied for the superintendency in Trenton, I explained in my application letter what had happened and the matter was never even discussed. Being demoted for standing on principle was not a liability.)

LEADING FOR LEARNING

In some respects, my experience as regional superintendent was among the most professionally rewarding of my career. I had a unique opportunity to focus on instructional improvement without needing to give much attention to operational concerns. I was able to design, invent, and build in ways that were directly responsive to problems that emerged from consideration of student achievement and descriptive data.

By taking an inquiry stance (see Cochran-Smith & S. L. Lytle, 2009), rather than a didactic one, I was able to invite the principals and regional office staff to challenge conventions and reposition our strategies for improving teaching and learning in our schools. When problems did arise—for example, the budget crisis—I could demonstrate that there were opportunities to teach even in crisis, by taking the same inquiry-based approaches we had used to address pedagogical issues.

As regional superintendent I was able to model several approaches to leading that I had come to believe could bring about sustainable improvement. The first was to take a deliberate approach to learning the context in which the principals and regional office staff worked, but to do this in a way that connected directly with the learning experiences of students in classrooms. The second was to demonstrate how one could lead by teaching, and to demonstrate pedagogies that were engaging and powerful. The third was to assume that among the principals, teachers, and regional office staff, we had sufficient intellectual and social capital to examine our practice and improve on it. The fourth was to demonstrate that organizational performance can improve over the long term when goals are relatively broad and nonspecific.

4

Principal, Again

I arrived as the new principal of University City High School (UCHS) in March 1995. The previous summer I had been demoted from a senior-level management position to my last tenured position, high school principal, because of strong ideological differences with a new superintendent. I had spent the previous eight months on "special assignment," a euphemism for being given a non-job and put, almost literally, in a closet. In my time at UCHS, I drew on all my previous leadership experience, as well as my teaching, reading, and writing, to bring about a dramatic turnaround in the school. The story of UCHS illustrates how I once again followed the pattern for approaching challenges that had served me so well over the years: learn and read the context, determine the work, begin the building process, keep track of progress, give feedback, and keep purpose in front of everything that is done.

BACK TO SCHOOL

Although I had been a principal before my arrival at University City, it had been almost fifteen years since I had worked in a school, and I had never been principal of a large, comprehensive high school. Now I was supposed to be the latest savior for a high school labeled by the *Philadelphia Daily News* as "a sea of chaos" (Bello, 1995, p. 3).

When I got there, UCHS had almost two thousand students, of whom 99 percent were African American and 92 percent were from low-income families. At least 10 percent had been involved with the criminal justice system, and about seventy-five of the students returned from incarceration each year. In addition, at least two hundred of the female students were teen mothers, and another two hundred would give birth in the coming year. During the school year, between 150 and 250 students were on "office roll," meaning that they had been absent for ten consecutive days or more and had to bring a parent or guardian to school to be readmitted. Combining transfers from other schools, returns from incarceration, disciplinary transfers, and readmits from office roll, ten to fifteen new or returning students were enrolled daily from October through May. Historically, fewer than 40 percent of the entering ninth graders would graduate. In terms of enrollment stability alone, the school was out of control.

For many years, University City had been perceived as the most disruptive and contentious high school in the city; students and staff spent each day in fear for their personal safety. The two principals who preceded me had each been removed from the school during spring break because the school was in such disarray. I was the fourth principal in a four-year interval and the first white principal the school had ever had. When I walked in on the Monday after spring break, the faculty and students had no idea that my predecessor had been removed and that I was their new principal. There was no planned transition. The perception of the staff was that I had been assigned to the school by the superintendent as a punishment. (In fact, I had asked months previously to be assigned to a school, but had been kept in escrow. Perhaps there had been a plan in this abrupt transition after all.)

During my first few months, I spent most of the school day walking the hallways and dropping into classrooms. I was conscious of a climate of tension fueled by the prospect of imminent fights. In the second floor atrium between five hundred and seven hundred students gathered during each class change, with street gangs congregating in the corners and other students watching the show from an overlooking balcony, all waiting for some spark to ignite mayhem.

I made a strategic decision. I was not Joe Clark and I was not going to be able to change the climate single-handedly. The best course seemed to be to pray that we could get though to the end of the school year without a serious incident, and put our energy into redesigning the entire school for the coming school year. I determined that successful redesign would require putting the people the kids trusted most as close to them as possible.

One thing I had learned in my hallway travels was that among our security officers and hallway monitors were a group of African American men and women who cared about the kids and understood how important it was for them to get a decent high school education. These were the ones who knew the kids best. Some were from the community; others knew the kids' brothers, cousins, aunts, and grandmothers. They were the ones the kids confided in and went to for help and counsel. And they had an array of life experiences—former state cop, professional musician, leader in the Masons, Sunday school teacher, closet intellectual—that hadn't been valued. Prior to my arrival, their roles had been as enforcers, clearing the hallways, chasing kids to class, breaking up fights, escorting miscreants to the discipline office. My sense was that this group needed to be near the center of our counseling and caretaking efforts.

ANOTHER BUDGET CRISIS, ANOTHER OPPORTUNITY

Within two weeks of my arrival, we were directed to cut the school's proposed $11 million budget by almost 10 percent to help resolve a districtwide financial crisis, so a demoralized and shell-shocked community was now being confronted with new leadership *and* a significant reduction in its resources. I decided to use the budget cut as an opportunity to help the school community clarify its priorities and generate "investment capital." By cutting 15 percent rather than 10 percent we could generate about $500,000 to support new programs—the extra cuts would create our venture capital fund.

The whole process was conducted publicly—no deals, no secrets. The entire community was invited to watch and participate as we tried to solve the problem. On a blackboard in a basement meeting room I laid out the detailed school budget, including salaries for all categories of positions, money for equipment, books, and supplies, and so forth. Then the school scheduling person and I listed the "roster comp" time for every teacher—that is, the number of course reductions teachers were granted so they could assume other duties. A dean of discipline might be teaching no classes and a department head three rather than five. If an average teacher salary, including benefits, was $75,000, that meant that each period was worth $15,000, and each "released" period had to provide a benefit of at least $15,000.

As we examined the school's resource utilization—dollars, people, time—we recognized that we were spending $1 million annually, 10 percent of our budget, on policing, safety, and discipline. We were running a prison, not a school, and we realized that if we didn't reallocate a substantial portion of those dollars to instruction we could not improve opportunities for learning.

I was well aware that the reductions would mean losing teachers and support staff, but I also knew that whoever was dropped was highly likely to find a job elsewhere in the district, so short-term pain for them could lead to long-term gain for the school. One example illustrates the process and highlights the value of my read-the-context approach. My hallway travels and informal conversations had given me a reasonable sense of school politics. And one thing I had learned was that the bulk of the faculty resented the three reading teachers, who had small classes and whose work seemed to make no appreciable difference in student reading skills. One of the three was the teachers' union representative for the school, but most of the faculty held him in low regard; they had elected him because no one else would do the job. Already we had identified $225,000 of the reductions we needed to make—we would eliminate the reading department.

We wanted to be equitable in making reductions in the sense that we didn't want all cuts to fall on any one group of employees. As an example, we dropped the vice principal for discipline and replaced her with a paraprofessional who was extraordinary in working with parents and kids, and saved $60,000 in the process.

By the time we had completed our analysis and identified reductions we could make, we had reached our target of $1 million and exceeded it by $500,000. We used the extra $500,000 to underwrite our reorganization plan: The school would be subdivided into six small learning communities, or schools-within-a-school, in which students would take all but their physical education classes. We were intentionally shifting the school's core organizing construct from heavy policing/subject/department to caring/support/personalization. We had also shifted from being resource-poor to resource-"rich" in the sense that we had money to spend on new programs, good ideas, and professional learning.

In the language of organizational sociology, we worked aggressively to increase our social and organizational capital. With money from our new venture capital fund we started a for-profit computer repair program built around a highly skilled teacher, and we were able to pay kids for their work. Another teacher had his own web page design business outside of school. We persuaded him to develop a counterpart within the school, bought the equipment, taught the kids how to use it, and started selling design services to other schools and small businesses. Using our contacts and networks, we sought out student internship opportunities in our community (which included a major research university and teaching hospital). And we invested heavily in technology to make us more efficient and increase our ability to communicate.

The teacher who did our school scheduling, Dave Kelter, was extraordinarily skilled and key in our designing and putting in place our small learning community organization. Recognizing his talents, I suggested to the school district central office that, for a fee, our leadership team would be willing to provide technical assistance to other high schools as they undertook similar reorganizations. Within a year we were earning $250,000, paid by charge-backs from other schools and added to our school's budget. For our school the additional funding was useful, but the symbolic importance of leading reform rather than being the perpetual doormat was even more important to our collective sense of efficacy.

BUILDING TRUST EVERY DAY

From their research on school performance, Bryk and Schneider (2003) concluded that relational trust among students, teachers, parents, and principals has a strong relationship to a school's success or failure. One of their observations was that "as individuals interact with one another around the work of schooling, they are constantly discerning the intentions embedded in the actions of others" (p. 41). I had had enough experience leading schools before I came to University City to know that everything I did every day, from the moment of my arrival until I left at the end of the day, would be observed and interpreted by students, employees, and parents. As principal, I was the big fish in the bowl. My ability to lead the school through the budget reduction, my presence in the hallways, and my respect for the support staff all contributed to establishing the trust I would need to take us farther.

What I call "The Coke Machine Incident" illustrates the value of cultivating trust. It began in the UCHS faculty mail room, which was adjacent to my office. A small sign on the outer door of the mail room said "NO Students," but because the door was one of two entrances to the school's main office, students occasionally passed through. In one corner was a Coke machine. One afternoon, just after school let out, an eleventh-grade girl entered the mail room and bought a can of Coke. As she turned to leave, one of the security staff, an African American matriarch, accosted her, grabbed for the Coke, and told her she didn't belong in the room. The student pushed back, and a brief scuffle ensued. I came out of my office to see what was going on and helped break up the confrontation. The security guard was furious and made it clear that she was going to pursue the matter. Later that afternoon, she went to the city police station and filed formal assault charges against the girl.

My investigation of the incident—getting statements from the two parties and from witnesses—indicated that the guard was at least as much at fault as the student. I advised the guard that if she insisted on taking the matter to court, I would appear as a witness for the student. Several weeks later, I was present for the scheduled court hearing, but the guard agreed to withdraw the charges just as the case was about to begin. The guard subsequently let it be known around the school that she blamed me for undermining her authority and potentially the discipline of the entire school. The truth was that the discipline climate had improved dramatically, and everyone knew it. I would like to think that part of the reason for the change was that the students were beginning to trust the school administration—because the adults were also being held to reasonable behavior standards.

PUBLIC SECTOR ENTREPRENEURSHIP: CAFETERIA TO FOOD COURT

One of the most troublesome locations in the school was the lunchroom, a warehouse-like space with institutional cafeteria tables with attached benches and a factory-line food service bay—and lousy food. The atmosphere in the cafeteria was always grim, fights were common, and students "cut" lunch rather than subject themselves to the chaos.

Because I had worked in the central office and had been a regional superintendent before becoming principal, I knew the administrators who ran Food Services for the district (my social capital) and knew that the district was experimenting with a new approach to feeding students. Because of my experience in the planning office, I also knew about Universal Feeding, a new federal program designed to increase student participation in subsidized meal programs and decrease the paperwork for qualification (my intellectual capital). The Food Services division wanted to try the program in a high school to see whether more students could be encouraged to participate, thereby generating more revenue. Through a combination of inveigling and badgering, I persuaded the Food Services hierarchy that our school would be an ideal place to experiment with a new food-court approach to meal service, modeled on a design used in malls and colleges.

Food Services agreed to make University City their experimental site, but the condition was that we would have to close the cafeteria for a year and feed the students in the auditorium. We discussed this option with the students and security staff, and all agreed that a daily menu of pizza was an acceptable price to pay for a new cafeteria (using our organizational capital). As construction progressed, we took students and staff on tours so they could see the prospective reward for their sacrifice.

When the new food court opened the following year, the students were amazed. Booths and tables created the ambiance of a family restaurant. And there were five food service counters, each offering a different cuisine—all free! Participation in the feeding program immediately tripled. The Food Services division was ecstatic. Behavior problems disappeared. And the food court became a symbol of our "new" school, a place where students felt respected and comfortable. This innovation in our feeding program was in fact a "high leverage" strategy leading to "a large outcome in terms of quality and/or quantity for a minimal investment of energy" (Hargreaves, 2003a, p. 5), markedly improving the school's learning environment.

INCREASING CAPITAL, OR THE SCHOOL AS A BIG BUS

Turning around a school, particularly a troubled inner-city high school, might be thought of as a process of building human capital (Hargreaves, 2003a), or getting the right people on the school bus and the wrong people off (Collins, 2001).

Getting the Right People On the Bus

There were two ways we built human capital at UCHS. One I have already touched on—learning about the underutilized or overlooked talents of people on our staff, and then building around them. Here are a few examples: Two of our security officers who were also outstanding professional musicians volunteered to work with our music teacher in developing a jazz band. Our school psychologist had a web design business; we built a high-end computer lab, he began teaching web design courses, and soon we had a student-operated small business of our own. A computer teacher started a Cisco-certified computer network training program and a computer building and repair shop; her students operated the business and were paid as hourly employees. The list goes on, but the moral of the story is clear. Learning about these hidden talents and then encouraging faculty and staff to use their talents for the benefit of our students was a quick and powerful way to build our capacity.

The other approach to building human capital was to recruit as high-powered a teaching and administrative team as we could. That meant using all my networks, and those of my colleagues, to encourage folks to come to University City. My experience had been that teachers and administrators want to work in schools where they feel valued and where they can experience success. I had an established reputation in the school district as an innovator and someone who respected teachers. As vacancies came up, I reached out to colleagues and friends, asking them to join us. Dina Portnoy, for example, had been a "teacher on special assignment," providing support for high school small learning communities across the district, but funding for her position had ended. She accepted a classroom position at UCHS teaching English and quickly became a favorite of the students for her high standards, high expectations, and let's-have-fun approach.

Three of our assistant principals moved on to become principals (with my encouragement and support), and each time one left I reached out to someone who would complement my strengths and could replace me if I were to leave. The last of these recruits, Flo Johnson, had been a counselor, social worker, and assistant principal at several middle and high schools, and she had worked with me at Pennsylvania Advancement School twenty years before. She was passionate about improving life chances for African American students and extraordinary at working with them and their parents (not my strong suit). When I left UCHS, she was the obvious choice to be the next principal and to keep the school on course.

Another recruit was Joe Youngblood. Joe had come to the Graduate School of Education at Penn as a doctoral student after completing law school in Iowa, and he had taken a course I was teaching during my sabbatical. Like Flo, he was deeply committed to improving opportunities for African American young people. I persuaded him to take a position as coordinator for the community learning program we were developing for our special education students. He organized and managed a program based at the University of Pennsylvania Hospital that was so successful I tell its story later in the chapter.

Getting the Right People Off the Bus

But it's not just getting the right people on board. One of my early mentors had taught me that as an administrator, and particularly as a principal, you define yourself by the people you fire or offload. One example illustrates the importance of taking action when it's warranted.

A trick I had learned as a central office administrator was to ask Human Resources for a W-2 (tax statement) run at the end of each tax year, with individuals rank-ordered by the total amount they had been paid for the year. (It's not unusual to find that a carpenter is making more than most principals.) As principal at University City, I asked for a W-2 run for the school faculty and staff and was stunned to find that one of our lead teachers had been paid $35,000 more than his base salary. I asked the district's controller to investigate, and learned that the teacher had listed himself on several different overtime payrolls—and on many occasions had submitted duplicate invoices. He had arranged to be paid from two or three different accounts for time worked on the same days.

This person was the teacher leader for one of our six small learning communities, health professions, but my sense was that he was more concerned about his personal status and recognition than about his students' success. Our school was only a few blocks away from one of the largest healthcare centers in the United States, yet he had made almost no effort to develop working relationships with the many and varied healthcare organizations in our neighborhood. Nor was he making an effort to mentor and counsel his community's students. Most of the faculty held him in low regard. His few allies were those he had rewarded with overtime pay. I initiated a formal evaluation process, which ended with his termination.

It's Not Just Employees On the Bus

Earlier I mentioned that we had ten to fifteen new or returning students being admitted or readmitted to school every day. As a neighborhood public school we were obligated to accept them, but the constant arrival of new students in their classes was a continuing problem for teachers. To reduce the disruption, we used part of our venture capital to set up a "portal class" to which we assigned the new admits. To become part of a small learning community, they had to attend for ten straight days; only then were they given a regular course schedule. Just this one simple adjustment made a big difference in increasing continuity and a sense of community.

Our Neighbor as a Source of Human Capital

We didn't consider our own faculty and staff as the sum total of our human resources. An obvious but underutilized resource was almost at our doorstep, the University of Pennsylvania, just a few blocks from the school campus. With help from the university's Center for Community Partnerships, we developed a series of courses for our students taught by university faculty, often with Penn students as tutors or co-equals with our students. A classics professor used ancient and modern graffiti as an entry point for ancient history. An anthropology professor had her class of university students, matched with an equal number of high school students, do ethnographies of each other's schools. An English professor had his Penn students act as teaching assistants in the high school's eleventh-grade English courses and coplanned his course with the high school teachers, using the same texts they would be teaching. Sometimes the courses met at the high school, sometimes on the university campus.

We also took every opportunity to bring in Penn undergraduates as tutors and mentors, and to recruit graduate school student teachers from the secondary education program at the Graduate School of Education. In building this relationship with the university we were dramatically increasing the intellectual, social, and organizational capital our students and teachers could access.

TO WHAT END?

So how did all of this come together to help us become an open, caring, innovative, trusting, and more effective school? I tried to answer that question in a paper I presented at the American Educational Research Association (AERA) Annual Meeting in 1998 (Lytle, 1998). For several years I had been reading the emergent literature on chaos and complexity, and in the AERA presentation I tried to show how chaos theory helped explain the relationship between what we had done and the school's marked improvement, citing Wheatley to argue,

> The potent force that shapes behavior in . . . fractal organizations . . . is the combination of simply expressed expectations of acceptable behavior and the freedom available to individuals to assert themselves in non-deterministic ways. Fractal organizations trust in the power of guiding principles or values, knowing that they are strong enough influences of behavior to shape every employee [and student] into a desired representative of the organization. (Wheatley, 1992, p. 132)

In practice, this meant:

- Listening to students who asked for help.
- Designing a student "handbook" that fit on a single 8.5 × 11 sheet of paper and had one sentence about "the rules."
- Making sure we had enough discretionary resources so that teachers or staff members could count on support for new ideas or needs.
- Letting new programs emerge from the faculty rather than implementing canned solutions from some corporate entity.

- Respecting nonprofessional staff and encouraging them to be teachers and counselors in informal (and sometimes formal) ways.
- Not screaming.
- Respecting the students' language, dress, and conventions.
- Helping with the dirty work.
- Advocating for students when adults were wrong.
- Listening, supporting, and encouraging.
- Trusting that there was more capacity in the faculty and staff than any of us knew.

Collectively we recognized that conventional linear planning was not workable in this setting. Instead, we proceeded on many fronts at once, recognizing that the sum of our efforts would be a more livable and effective school.

Three years later, parents were lined up to get their kids into the school instead of transferring them out. Discipline problems were sharply reduced, graduation rates had risen by 64 percent, mildly handicapped students were in regular classes, test scores were up, and course failures were down. Students were reporting being cared about by teachers and support staff, and faculty morale was high. The superintendent (he who had demoted me) acknowledged that University City exemplified what was possible within the constraints of limited resources, a restrictive teachers' contract, and a desperately needy community.

Evidence Feeds Improved Performance

But there's more to the University City story—which perhaps helps explain how this all works. During my first year at UCHS, false fire alarms and bomb threats were daily occurrences; by my third year, there were none the entire year. Through a careful analysis of district records, I was able to demonstrate that our school received proportionately more students transferring in from incarceration than any other high school in the city, but we also had a lower request rate for disciplinary transfers of our own students than any comparable high school. Attendance and suspension data showed marked improvement. Our dropout (attrition) rate had dropped, enrollment had increased, and the graduation rate had improved, again markedly.

The data we collected indicated that we were taking far better care of our students than any of our peer schools. We were building relational trust, and we were at a point where we could concentrate on improving teaching and learning. That is something both our students and their parents recognized. And there was an important concomitant: We were collecting and analyzing the data and monitoring our performance ourselves, not leaving it to the central office or the state to decide whether we were becoming a better school. As our students, their parents, and our staff saw the evidence of our continuing improvement, their confidence grew—success bred more success.

Perhaps the highlight of my last year at University City was attending a graduation ceremony in the courtyard of the University of Pennsylvania Hospital. The ceremony had been planned by a group of students who had spent the year interning at the hospital—as mail clerks, food service workers, nurse's assistants, and in other support jobs. Their teachers had also been based at the hospital, so the students took their core subject classes in a hospital meeting room. They had also gotten tutoring and mentoring support from Penn undergraduates.

For the graduation, the students had designed and printed the programs, organized the refreshments, invited the hospital staff they had worked with, and arranged for the speakers, several of whom were their peers. Their parents and siblings were there in force, and the ceremony couldn't have been a more perfect celebration.

The kicker was that these were all special education students who had been written off back in elementary school and had now found a place for themselves in the world. In fact, many of them were going to continue on at the hospital as full-time employees. What had I done? Not much, other than to give the teachers permission to organize this off-site program and then support them whenever they asked for assistance. But that didn't diminish my sense of satisfaction in seeing the pride of the graduates.

Building Capital, Increasing Equity, Improving Performance

As I mentioned in the Introduction, one of Rick Hess's challenges to me when he suggested that I write this book was to demonstrate how school leaders can be entrepreneurial in what appear to be conventional and traditional organizational settings. I would like to think that the story of UCHS provides a compelling illustration of what's possible even when the conditions seem less than ideal.

One way to interpret what happened at University City is to return to David Hargreaves's definitions of intellectual, social, and organizational capital:

> Intellectual Capital—"education and training of individuals, . . . [including] knowledge, skills, capabilities, competencies, talents, expertise, practices and routines." (2003a, p. 4)

In the instance of University City, exploiting intellectual capital meant learning about and then putting to good use the many talents and capabilities of every employee, regardless of formal job titles and position descriptions. It meant investing in the learning of our current employees and attracting highly qualified replacements when vacancies occurred. It also meant creating the conditions that would attract and make good use of the enormous intellectual resources of the University of Pennsylvania, only blocks away.

> Social Capital—"the degree of trust that exists between the members and stakeholders, . . . the extent and quality of the networks between its members and its external partners. Organisations that are rich in social capital have a strong sense of themselves as a community." (Hargreaves, 2003a, p. 5)

Employing social capital was the most difficult challenge at University City because, at the time of my arrival, the sense of threat and conflict was omnipresent. Leadership in this regard meant spending much of my time in public space, observing, connecting, intervening, and supporting—not presuming that climate management was other people's work. It also meant reorganizing the school into small learning communities that would increase the connections among adults, between adults and students, and among students (e.g., taking pride in being part of the "Law & Justice" community). As these communities stabilized, our external partners were more willing to contribute their time and effort.

> Organisational Capital—"the knowledge and skill about how to change the school by making better use of its intellectual and social capital to produce high leverage strategies of teaching and learning." (Hargreaves, 2003a, p. 6)

Our organizational capital increased as we moved from a traditional, departmentalized, comprehensive high school to a set of small learning communities, as we moved from a conventional forty-five-minute-period schedule to block scheduling, when we eliminated the bell system and let teachers keep time, when we introduced the portal class to minimize the disruptions caused by constant student entry and re-entry, when we began an after-school program for overaged dropouts, when we shifted our staff utilization from discipline and control to instructional support, when we created engaging "hothouse" programs such as the computer repair company, and when we started a consulting business to make use of our capabilities (thereby generating revenue for the school and demonstrating that we didn't need help; rather, we were in a position to give help).

Financial and Facilities Capital—the more traditional definitions of capital.

In explaining how we dealt with a 10 percent, $1 million budget reduction, and in the process generated $500,000 in venture capital, I have told part of the story of how we went about underwriting the cost of reform. Eating pizza in the auditorium for a year so that we could have a fabulous new food court was another part. Yet another part of our success story was generating $250,000 in my third year from our consulting company, money we could reinvest in our own development. We couldn't have built our intellectual, social, and organizational capital to the degree we did if we hadn't also generated financial capital.

LEARNING TO LEAD, AGAIN

By the time I arrived at University City, I was experienced and mature enough to understand, as Barry Jentz and Jerry Murphy (2005b) say, that I needed to "hit the ground learning," not hit the ground running. I needed to "get on the balcony" (Heifetz & Linsky, 2002, p. 51) and give myself time to understand what was happening before I began to act. I couldn't intervene in ways that would help solve the school's diverse and endemic problems without first taking time to understand who we were and why the school was so chaotic.

I needed to begin by behaving in ways that communicated my respect for everyone—the support staff, the kids, and the faculty. I also needed to remind the community that our purpose was to ensure that every entering student left prepared for college, work, or military service or any combination of these.

There was another important principle I was guided by. Urban neighborhood schools have to teach every student who comes through the door; you don't get to choose. Similarly, at University City we needed to demonstrate that every employee could contribute to our mission, and we had an obligation to help employees contribute according to their talents. We had to model in dealing with the adult community how we expected the adults to deal with the student community. That didn't mean we would succeed with every student, or every employee, but it did mean that we had to make every possible effort for every individual.

And we needed to change school culture by learning to say yes instead of no. We had to have the resources to support experimentation and reward extraordinary effort. We needed to be a "can do" organization, not one making excuses by blaming the kids and the school system. Most importantly, we needed to help students see a manageable pathway to graduation, not focus on their failures.

I hope this account of my time as principal at UCHS answers the question, "Why lead?" In its most basic form, the answer is this: Because there is work to be done, and there is deep satisfaction in being able to help a school and a community become demonstrably better places. During my first few months at the school, there were daily interruptions and emergencies; my last year, there were none. My first year, we worked hard to keep kids in class; my last year, students would stop by the office to complain when a teacher wasn't doing a good job—they wanted me to do something about it. And as I recounted in the story about the graduation ceremony at the Penn Hospital, our seniors were leaving with a sense of pride, accomplishment, and direction.

TRANSITION

The irony of this story is that it was my demotion from an assistant superintendent position and reassignment as principal at University City that led to my appointment as superintendent in Trenton, New Jersey. As University City became increasingly successful, our consulting business grew—helping other high schools reorganize into small learning communities and implementing block scheduling. It was in this context that we were contacted by representatives of Trenton Central High School. A few of us went to Trenton and assisted in a workshop there; then a group from Trenton came to visit us, including two board members. They liked what they saw and experienced, and they were especially impressed by how cordial the students were. Shortly after the visit I was invited to become a candidate for the Trenton superintendency.

When I was offered the position a few months later, I was torn because I knew there was more work to be done at University City. But I was also aware that Trenton posed more substantial challenges. And I considered my long-term prospects for a return to senior management in Philadelphia to be nil.

In retrospect, I am virtually certain that if I had still been a central office administrator at the time I became a candidate for the Trenton superintendency, I would not have been selected—I would have been just another white administrator in an urban district. It was my work at University City that persuaded the Trenton board that I was for real. It was seeing the school that sold the board on me, not my résumé. But that only got me the job. The board was taking a risk. I had never been a superintendent, although I had held every other position in the usual progression path. I had the technical and political skills the job required. But the deep question was whether I had the courage and the will to take on Trenton.

The Pennsylvania Advancement School, the Intensive Learning Center, the Parkway Program, the research and planning office, my "sabbatical" at Penn, and my regional superintendency had all provided opportunities for me to learn. But UCHS had been my first real test at turning around a troubled urban school. Now the question was whether I could take these lessons to scale in Trenton, a district in desperate need of a turnaround.

I think what I learned from University City is that I *did* have what it takes to engineer a turnaround, but that it was not something I could do single-handedly. I knew when I went there that it was a mess. And I knew that there were no quick solutions. I also knew that I could stand in the hallways and scream at the kids, but that wasn't going to make anything better (and, besides, they'd laugh). I had never dealt directly with an organization in crisis before my arrival at University City, and the only way it was going to get better was if I provided the leadership to make it happen. With my encouragement, two of our assistant principals had sought and been promoted to principalships during my tenure. But given my many previous experiences with planned and unplanned leadership transitions, I had been careful to recruit and develop prospective successors, and knew when I accepted the superintendent appointment that the school would be in good hands.

As I headed for Trenton I understood that I was moving into another situation beyond my zone of experience, and that once again there were no fast solutions. I might have been arrogant or confident enough to tackle Trenton or a similar superintendency direct from my central office position, but having been re-immersed in the day-to-day reality of school was what provided the compass I needed to navigate the challenges of Trenton. University City was my finishing school. It taught me how to use my accumulated experience and learning to invent and improvise solutions that worked for kids, how to increase capital as a school improvement strategy, and how to be a public sector entrepreneur.

II

CHANGING STATES

Superintendent, Trenton, New Jersey

5

Learning the Context

My eight years as superintendent in Trenton, New Jersey, was a test of all I believed and all I had learned. As I recount how I approached this new position, how my role changed as leadership challenges shifted over time, and how I continued to learn about leading, elements of my "theory of practice" once again reveal themselves:

- Learn and read the context.
- Determine the work to be done and the pace for doing it. Take an inquiry stance.
- Build human, social, organizational, and intellectual capital.
- Create an organizational culture that encourages and supports risk, inquiry, and entrepreneurship.
- Question convention and current practice.
- Rather than solve problems, set problems for others to solve.
- Monitor, track, and evaluate.
- Celebrate accomplishments and provide feedback.
- Reflect, make sense of situations, and stay centered.
- Be clear about purpose and keep it in the forefront.

ENTRY: TRENTON LEARNS ABOUT ME

I knew something about the situation in Trenton from work our University City High School (Philadelphia) consulting company had done with Trenton Central High School. A consultant I knew who had also worked with the Trenton district encouraged me to apply for the superintendent position there because she felt I had the attributes the job required. Although there was more work I wanted to do at University City, I was intrigued by the possibilities of leading a relatively small urban district.

During my candidacy I had looked at newspapers, driven around the city, and made an effort to get a better sense of the challenges I would face. The representative of the district's search firm was helpful in further acquainting me with those challenges and in sketching the political context. Two interviews with the Trenton Board of Education had given me a sense of what their concerns were and what they saw as priorities. Because the district was such a mess, the mayor had given serious consideration to a takeover in which he would control the district and appoint a chief executive officer, but he had been persuaded by the state's commissioner of education to try one more time with a conventional superintendent appointment. Because Trenton's school board was appointed by the mayor, he could influence how the selection process played out.

Final Interview and Selection

To make sure the press didn't learn who the three finalists were, the last round of interviews for the position was conducted in Princeton, one of New Jersey's wealthiest communities, an irony that gave me some pause. I had brought with me a portfolio of artifacts and reports from my administrative career in Philadelphia, but most of them stayed in my carrying bag. The board members' questions were generally predictable, and I felt I had answered them in a satisfactory way. But one question was posed as a "case": What if a swimming teacher at a school left the pool while students were in it, resulting in a near-drowning? Further, what if the principal of the school reacted to the incident in a way that compromised the district's ability to discipline the teacher? I responded that the case didn't sound fictional to me, which produced knowing nods from several members of the board.

When the interview ended, the board president thanked me and told me the decision would be made the following Monday evening. He would call me by 9:00 p.m. to let me know whether I had been selected. Monday evening passed without a call, and at 11:00 I told my wife that someone else had apparently gotten the job and we might as well go to bed. At 11:30, when I was already sound asleep, the phone rang. It was the board president, announcing that I had been named as Trenton's new superintendent. I was stunned.

My Introduction as Superintendent

At the time I was named superintendent (actually "Chief School Administrator" in Trenton parlance) in June 1998, I was well aware that

I would be Trenton's first white superintendent in more than twenty years and that the mayor (African American) had taken a political risk in supporting me. On the evening of my formal appointment, as I sat in a side room waiting to be introduced, the board met until after midnight while the president, unbeknownst to me, tried to cajole a recalcitrant member into voting for my appointment so as to make it unanimous. At one point, the board's attorney appeared and asked whether I would be willing to accept the position at $15,000 less than the advertised salary. Figuring that if I compromised on my first decision, I would face a continuing series of pressures to compromise, I said no. Eventually the opposition member (who had supported another candidate) backed down, the board voted unanimously, and we all shared a moment of triumph.

Managing the Symbol System

The board was determined that my contract contain performance incentives to give them leverage in upcoming negotiations with teachers and administrators. I wasn't opposed to bonus provisions, but I was very uncomfortable with the notion that I stood to gain as much as $30,000 annually for work that was being done by teachers, principals, and support staff. I suggested a compromise. I would agree to the bonus provision on the condition that 80 percent of whatever I earned was put in a "last dollar" scholarship fund for graduating seniors. The board agreed, and over the next six years the total contribution amounted to well over $100,000.

My contract also provided that I have use of an automobile; I opted for one from the motor pool. I took a used desk for my office and put it in a corner facing the window so that I would never be sitting behind a desk when I met with visitors. The only furniture I ordered were file cabinets and bookcases. My wife and I bought a townhouse in a neighborhood close to the city center, prompting a newspaper article. Through a series of entry decisions, I was intentionally managing the symbols surrounding the arrival of a new superintendent, and signifying my commitment to the city and its children.

Checking Me Out

As I have noted, my first contact with Trenton had come through a consulting business we had set up when I was principal of University City High School in Philadelphia. At one point in that relationship, a group of Trenton teachers, parents, and board members had visited University City and had been impressed with the climate, particularly the way students had greeted them as they toured the school. So some in the district already had a sense that maybe I was for real, and that I had been able to lead an inner-city high school not much different from Trenton Central High. When I was named as superintendent, the Trenton underground went into action immediately. Trenton folks called their contacts in Philly to see what the word was on me. Some shared what they had heard—that I was regarded as someone who was serious about improving schools for minority kids and had done good work. That made my transition a whole lot easier.

LEARNING THE DISTRICT CONTEXT

The Mayor and the Clergy

In learning the context in Trenton, I had a tutor. By supporting my appointment as superintendent, Trenton's mayor, Doug Palmer, had not only taken a political risk, but as an African American he was violating an implicit community norm that only black candidates could provide suitable leadership in the city. A few weeks after my arrival, the mayor arranged a breakfast meeting with the city's black clergy to introduce me. In many respects they were the city's elders, and he knew that I would need their support if I was going to be successful.

After the usual pleasantries, he told the story of his interviewing me. As one of three finalists I had been asked to meet him at his home so that the media would not be aware that he was interviewing the candidates. I arrived at his house, was greeted at the door by his administrative assistant, and accompanied her to the living room, where I could hear him on the telephone in another room. A few minutes later he walked in, we shook hands, and then we talked for two hours about my background, how I would approach the job, and what the challenges were in the city. When I left, he was noncommittal.

Trenton's Board of Education is appointed by the mayor; I obviously got the job, and what the mayor may have said to the board I do not know, although he claimed he never intervened in their decision. But, as he told the assembled clergy that morning, his reaction when he walked into the room to interview me was, "Holy shit, he's white!" It had never occurred to him that the search committee would send forward a white candidate as a finalist. In telling this story to this group, the mayor was doing several things—certifying that I was the right one for the job, that I could be trusted even though I was not black, and that I should be able to count on their support. He was also making clear to me, without saying so, that I would need to work with this group if I was going to accomplish what he and I hoped for the district and the city. He knew well that social capital matters.

The Fishbowl

Because I was appointed as superintendent in late June, I had until September to learn as much about the district as I could before the school year got under way. I did the conventional things—reviewed the budget, read the teachers' contract, looked at school performance data, and drove around the city. But I also wanted to understand how parts of the district worked: budget development, food services, special education, federal programs, transportation, maintenance, and so on. I considered interviewing the heads of each division and thought it might be interesting to invite others to sit in on the meetings. As I consulted with the folks in the central office, that idea quickly morphed into a more elaborate plan. Why not use these discussions as an opportunity for anyone in the district or community who was interested to learn along with me?

We decided to use the central office auditorium as the meeting place, and arranged the seats in a semicircle with a small table at the center. Each division director would begin with a brief presentation, and we would talk about the strengths and challenges of the division while an audience listened to our discussion. After forty-five minutes or an hour, I would open up the discussion to questions and comments from anyone in the audience. The schedule of topics would be publicized, and since we had a citywide cable television channel, we would televise the meetings as well.

The meetings quickly became a hit. Board members, city council members, community activists, parents, teachers, principals, and union leaders attended. Not only was I learning a great deal about the district, but so was everybody else. Much to my amazement, I began to hear from people who were watching the meetings on television.

The *Trenton Times* ran a series of stories on the meetings, culminating in an editorial on "The 'Fishbowl' Strategy," which, it explained, was

> designed to let the public observe and comment as the superintendent and senior staff examined the complex workings of the district . . . a shrewd move on Lytle's part to let employees and district residents join him as he saw Trenton's beleaguered district for the first time. . . . "Let's see what's here so we can move on together" seems to be the message. (Editorial, *Trenton Times*, August 28, 1998, p. 10)

One of my colleagues observed:

> These "tutoring" sessions for the new superintendent did several things: they modeled a learning attitude on his part, informed many people about the complexity of the school district, quickly developed trust in the new leader because he was able to demonstrate competence and collegiality in these sessions, and communicated transparency as a value to relevant stakeholders. The sessions also gave the superintendent a sense of the capabilities of key staff, the concerns of the community, and the challenges and opportunities the district was facing. (Sanaghan & Lytle, 2008, p. 3)

In telling this story I am not suggesting that the fishbowl process would be appropriate in every community or situation. But I am making the point that taking time to learn the context *before* starting to act has a great deal to do with how future decisions will be made, perceived, understood, and enacted.

Meeting the Principals

For me, a key in the early months of my superintendency was to establish a relationship between leading and teaching. My primary vehicle was the biweekly meetings of principals, and in the first year I did not invite central office administrators (other than the deputy superintendent) to attend. I wanted to make clear that in my view the principals were the key leadership group in implementing state-mandated reforms and improving organizational performance.

My sense emerging from the fishbowl meetings and my discussions with central office personnel was that the central office had dominated the schools for years and that, as a result, principals did not see themselves as leaders in the district. Central office oversight and centralized decision processes had fostered a dependency relationship that made principals managers but not leaders. My experience in Philadelphia suggested a contrary view: Teachers and parents looked to principals for leadership; the central office was a distant and forbidding place. I needed to get a sense of how the Trenton principals approached leading their schools as quickly as possible.

At my first meeting with them I said with a straight face, "This is simple. The district has lost 25 percent of its enrollment to charter schools. Our per-pupil cost is about $12,000. A private for-profit company, Noble Learning, has developed an effective model for operating schools at $6,500 per student. I'm going to offer Noble the chance to take over the district at their current cost. With 12,000 students currently on roll I should net about $5,000 per student, so I'm going to pay myself $60 million for organizing the takeover. And you'll all be unemployed." That got their attention.

Then we started talking in earnest about why the charter schools had been so successful. Mixed in with disparaging remarks were some important insights. The charters opened at 7:00 a.m. and closed at 6:00 p.m. with beginning- and end-of-day child care. They required uniforms. They didn't tolerate misbehavior. They had national partners like EdisonLearning, Inc. to provide support. They had "stolen" some of the district's best teachers and administrators.

So now we were ready to talk about what we were going to need to do improve our services and regain "market share." The inquiry was under way.

Visiting Schools

In earlier chapters, I have described how I went about learning the context at Parkway Program, the Northwest Region, University City High School, and each job I have held. In Trenton I took a similar approach. As soon as school opened in September, I was off touring schools. My practice was to get to at least two schools each morning. I would go to the main office, sign in on the visitor's register, ask the secretary to see the principal, and then take a walking tour of the building with the principal as guide. As we walked, I would ask for commentary on classrooms we entered or passed, and I would observe how the principal interacted with teachers, support staff, and the students. I didn't have a checklist or a rubric. That wasn't the point. I wasn't trying to evaluate the school's programs. Rather, I was constructing my own understanding of how each principal and how the group of principals approached their work.

Trenton Central High School as a Focal Point

My school tours confirmed an analysis I had made in reviewing data about our high school. Almost 70 percent of incoming ninth graders left before graduation, an appalling statistic. For that reason, during my first several months I spent a good deal of time at the high school, walking the halls, talking to teachers and administrators, observing and chatting with students, attending planning meetings, doing whatever I could to get a feel for the school. Although the administration, faculty, and staff were in the third year of developing a strategic plan to put the school on a new and improved course, it was apparent to me that they were in no hurry to change things. As far as they were concerned, they were doing what needed to be done, and if the students weren't taking advantage of their opportunities, then so be it. But the mayor and I saw the situation differently, and we wanted to increase the high school completion rate and reduce attrition.

When I had first met the mayor during the superintendent selection process, he'd been clear that reducing dropouts was his first priority. He also knew many of the staff members and parents at Trenton High and had a good sense of how troubled the school was. I understood that I would have his support for whatever reforms we needed to undertake to rectify long-standing problems, but I also recognized that it would be important to keep him informed about changes at the high school so that he could anticipate backdoor appeals and complaints.

LEARNING THE COMMUNITY

I also took the obligatory steps to establish ties to the Trenton community—I went to the Rotary meeting, met with the directors of social service agencies, attended the monthly public library board meetings, attended school parent meetings, and dropped in at political fundraising events. People were pleased to see me, pleased with what they had heard and read about me, and were generally encouraging. Each month I met with the mayor to review what I was doing and where I was headed.

Board Meetings

There is an enormous difference between attending school board meetings as a member of the superintendent's support team and being the superintendent. The superintendent is the board's sole employee; all other employees in the district work at the direction of the superintendent. The board is supposed to represent the community in providing direction for the district, but it also has extensive authority under state law because it must confirm everything from budgets and expenditures to personnel appointments, program review, and student trips.

The superintendent prepares the agenda for the board meetings, which is in large part driven by the need to seek the board's approval for the wide range of activities and decisions the operations of the district require. Depending on the superintendent's relationship with the board president and the board as a whole, agenda development may also involve the board.

And here I was. In the space of two months I had moved from the hallways of University City High School to the center of the platform on which the board met, looking down at the audience below.

I was fortunate to have Abdul Malik Ali as board president. Ali was the imam for Trenton's mosque, a former state prison guard, a long-time parent activist, and a product of the inner city. Most important, he had a deep commitment to improving opportunities for Trenton's children. He was an extremely skilled facilitator who could manage disparate personalities and issues with grace, guiding the board to consensus.

President Ali and I quickly established an easy rapport. He provided me informal counsel, and we worked collaboratively to put the Trenton schools on a constructive path.

Dealing with the Eight-Hundred-Pound Gorilla, the State

To this point, everything I have said about learning Trenton would suggest that the city was an independent and isolated enclave, wholly autonomous and independent. All I would need to do was learn my way around and pay attention to the school board, and then I would understand how to go about leading change and reform in the city schools. But that would be far, far from the truth. About 85 percent of the district's funding came from the state, the district had repeatedly been in trouble with the state Department of Education (DOE), and a recent state Supreme Court decision had dramatically increased the state's role and responsibility for improving urban schools. To be an effective superintendent, I knew I was going to have to master the state policy environment and develop working relationships with the DOE.

IMPLEMENTATION OF A COURT MANDATE

Although I was not aware of it when I applied for the superintendency, I quickly learned that Trenton was one of thirty "Abbott" districts in the state. Three New Jersey cities—Newark, Jersey City, and Patterson—have gotten a good deal of national attention as early examples of state takeover districts, but much less has been written about Abbott, the consent decree entered into by Governor Christie Whitman's administration (through the attorney general's office and the state DOE) and the New Jersey Supreme Court in May 1998. The consent agreement was the culmination of *Abbott v. Burke*, a series of equity cases spanning over twenty years during which the plaintiffs pressed the court to address long-standing shortcomings in the state's urban school districts, ranging from financial parity to program and facility inequities.

The importance of this consent decree is that it committed New Jersey to urban school reform far more directly than any other state in the union. (Many states have gained notice for whole-state reform efforts [e.g., Kentucky, California, Texas, and Tennessee], but only New Jersey has focused education reform in its urban districts. In the New Jersey experience, there is also a powerful object lesson for states and districts dealing with the corrective action and intervention provisions of the No Child Left Behind Act.)

I began working in Trenton on almost precisely the day on which the DOE issued the new Abbott regulations, its set of directives to the thirty districts. This first set of regulations included implementation deadlines for each of the major components of the Abbott decree and specifications for required submissions. Each component was elaborated in subsequent DOE plan and budget documents. Statewide orientation meetings were held in mid-September to introduce the regulations and planning requirements to superintendents and other district representatives.

The only practical way for me to make sense of what was happening was to start from the premise that the state, in effect, was taking over *all thirty* of the affected districts and was engaged, or, more accurately, enmeshed in an attempt to manage and micromanage reform in all of them simultaneously. The state's commitment of additional financial support to urban districts had already been substantial, and full implementation of Abbott, as the consent decree required, was likely to lead to extraordinary expenditures. The framing consideration was whether these massive infusions of money and the concomitant shifts in urban school district governance from local boards to the DOE would result in demonstrable benefits to students. If New Jersey failed in this effort, the conclusion would be drawn that increased funding for urban schools is not a sound investment. I was well aware that the stakes were extraordinarily high, and that I needed to be a careful student of the Abbott regulations and provisions.

Abbott Components

As I considered the Abbott regulations, I recognized that several of the components of the consent decree would directly determine the reforms we could undertake in Trenton. These are described in the sections that follow.

Parity Aid

The most important component, in terms of funding, was the agreement on parity aid in the state subsidy formula. All New Jersey districts are ranked on a ten-point scale in terms of ability to pay for public education. The parity aid agreement required that the thirty Abbott districts be funded at the same per-pupil expenditure level as the wealthiest districts in the two top ranks, a provision that produced an immediate benefit for Trenton and all Abbott districts. (This approach did not cap expenditures in wealthy districts, but it did mean that when their costs increased—for example, through a teacher contract settlement—wealthy communities would be obligated to pay for increased subsidies for the Abbott districts.)

Supplemental Funding

Where parity aid proved insufficient to implement the required components of Abbott, districts were entitled to apply for supplemental funds, both for preschool and for K–12 programs and services. One of the most difficult problems in implementing Abbott was that the court and the DOE, perhaps for different reasons, were persuaded by their expert witness that New Jersey urban schools already had sufficient funds (when Title I and other categorical funds were included) to implement the Abbott provisions without additional funding. This argument assumed that by eliminating assistant principals, counselors, paraprofessionals, and other staff, schools would save enough money to pay for the mandated components of Abbott, an argument that proved naïve and fallacious.

The result was that the DOE provided no additional funding for the implementation of Abbott in its fiscal year (FY) 1999 (1998–1999) or FY 2000 budgets. Despite this decision on the DOE's part, the Trenton Public Schools received $13.5 million in supplemental aid for FY 2000 through an aggressive appeal process. (The state's unwillingness to fully fund Abbott led Trenton, in concert with the Education Law Center, to bring suit against the DOE four times during my superintendency.)

Preschool

Abbott required that all three- and four-year-olds living in urban districts have access to free preschool, independent of family income. However, the governor's office determined that districts could *not* expand existing preschool programs to meet this requirement. Rather, program expansion had to be done through approved community providers, both profit and nonprofit (but not sectarian).

Whole School Reform

The court took the lead in insisting that all urban schools must adopt "research-based," comprehensive school reform models within a three-year period. For elementary schools, eight models were approved (e.g., Modern Red School House, Comer), and Success for All was made the default model. Schools failing to choose a model within the mandated time frame were required to implement Success for All. The court held that there were no demonstrably successful models at the secondary school level, so secondary schools were given somewhat greater latitude in selecting school improvement programs, although national models (e.g., Coalition for Essential Schools, Talent Development) were clearly preferred by the DOE.

Class Size Reduction

Abbott regulations stipulated that preschool classes not exceed teacher/student ratios of 1:15. For grades K–3, the ratio was 1:21; for grades 4–8, the ratio was 1:23; and for grades 9–12, the ratio was 1:24.

School Management Teams

All schools were required to form school management teams (SMTs) with equal numbers of teachers and parents; the principal was an *ex officio* member and the swing vote. The SMT was given direct authority over selection of the comprehensive school reform model and approval of the school budget.

School-Based Budgeting

Abbott regulations required that all schools involved in implementing comprehensive school reform models develop their own budgets using a zero-based approach. During fall 1999, representatives of the DOE worked directly with SMTs in developing their budgets, using standardized "illustrative budgets" in combination with DOE Abbott regulations to determine what staffing, professional development, and other resources schools would require to fully implement their chosen whole school reform models.

The time frame was extraordinarily tight, requiring Board of Education approval by late December. As a result, there was little time for meaningful review. Because the DOE had been so heavily criticized for its management of this process the previous year, their involvement at the school level tended to be primarily supportive; budgets were allowed that provided for staffing and other expenditures well beyond those of the previous year.

A key DOE decision was that the reduced class sizes featured in Success for All Schools, with 1:8 ratios during reading periods, and with certified teachers as tutors, would also be applied to elementary schools that had chosen different reform models, even when the model (e.g., Accelerated Schools) did not require smaller classes or added staffing. (Apparently, the DOE was afraid of creating resource inequities across whole school reform models.) The result was a dramatic increase in the prospective cost of Abbott implementation. (In Trenton, we understood the implications of the DOE's decision and hurried to implement it before they figured out what they had wrought.)

Core Content Curriculum Standards

The Abbott decision took as a first premise that students in the urban districts must be provided the educational conditions that would allow them to meet the state's core curriculum content standards. These standards include not only the basic subjects, but also the arts, health, physical education, and workplace readiness skills. Students must be provided appropriate instruction in all of these areas. As a result, "special" programs such as the arts could not be sacrificed to provide funding and time for remediation and basic skills (as has been the case in many cities across the country).

School Facilities

The court determined that urban students are entitled to schools that provide the conditions that make learning possible, and thus ordered new construction and rehabilitation to ensure adequate and appropriate school facilities. Because the core curriculum content standards require arts, science, technology, health, and physical education, the court determined that urban schools must include gyms, art rooms, music rooms, computer labs, and (in secondary schools) science labs.

Accountability

Schools and districts were to be held to account for full implementation of the Abbott mandates, although they had the option of beginning immediately or waiting for the second- or third-year cycles. (In Trenton, we were determined to get to the front of the line before the money ran out.) State tests administered in grades 3, 8, and 11 were stipulated as the measures of student achievement.

Varied Reactions to Abbott

Despite the prospect of substantial added resources, many of the Abbott districts saw the new regulations as an unwarranted intrusion in their programs and governance. Many of the individuals were put off by the orientation meetings. They believed they were already implementing effective programs, and they were reluctant to modify them. They didn't trust the DOE to provide the funding and support that implementing the court order would require, and decided to stall while they waited to see whether this would become just another unfunded mandate. These districts tended to postpone implementation of the Abbott programs until the third (i.e., the last possible) year.

As I considered the Abbott order and the newly issued directives from the DOE and discussed these policies with the advocates who had pressed the case, my sense was that, for Trenton, Abbott presented an extraordinary opportunity. If we were aggressive in implementing the order, we would have the leverage and resources we needed to drive reform and bring about the improvements the mayor, the board, and I all wanted. I saw my job as teaching the board, our employees, parents, elected officials, and the community about Abbott's potential. To keep it simple, I developed a one-page "picture" of the components of Abbott that I used to help our stakeholders understand why we should seize the moment.

ONWARD

By January of my first year, I had established my relationship with the Board of Education and the principals, learned the policy framework that would shape our efforts at reform, developed a preliminary understanding of the district, begun learning the community and developing networks and relationships, and sought guidance and counsel from the mayor. The board president and I were on the same page. It was time to get to work.

6

Determining the Work

My study of the context of the Trenton school system during my first months in the district, combined with Abbott imperatives, presented me with no shortage of issues in need of prompt attention. I had learned that the district had a very poor relationship with the Department of Education (DOE) and was just emerging from a period of intensive state oversight. The district was losing enrollment to a contingent of newly opened charter schools, and was in deep difficulty because of special education program compliance problems. We had a severe dropout problem. The mayor, the Board of Education, parents, the media, the community, and even the district's employees had lost confidence in the district's ability to provide safe and effective schooling. And, to top it all, we had massive Abbott implementation to undertake.

TRENTON'S APPROACH TO REFORM

Given the size and complexity of the task ahead, one might reasonably assume that we would have developed an enormous organizational chart or schedule to track each component. But that isn't how it actually happened. Instead, we kept talking about the many elements of the change, and in the process determined who would assume leadership for each piece and make it happen. The conversations included employee organization leaders, principals, central office administrators, and the board. The designs were emergent; the strategy was systemic in the sense that we were redesigning policies, practices, and components as we saw them bearing on each other.

For example, we realized that if we took advantage of the opportunity provided by Abbott to expand preschool, we would build a tremendous amount of goodwill with parents and with the community organizations that would operate the new or expanded preschool programs. At the same time, we could use the expanded preschools to counter the negative impact of charter schools on our enrollment while rebuilding our "brand." And, if we were going to successfully implement the comprehensive school reform models, we would need to work with our teachers' association in redesigning their contract in ways that would support increased teacher leadership in schools and more time for teachers to talk about implementation.

In looking back at what we had to do, the list seems overwhelming:

- Build and rebuild confidence: Overcome victimization, learned helplessness, defeatism, blaming, acceptance, suspicion, and isolation.
- Comply with all particulars of the Abbott decree.
- Increase high school completion (redesign the high school, add new programs).
- Align our curriculum with state standards.
- Improve school performance (as measured by state tests).
- Implement preschool.
- Increase market share (enrollment).
- Improve school climate.
- Increase organizational capacity where required—finance, special education, human resources, technology—while creating a culture in which the central office serves schools.
- Redesign governance: the board, school management teams, and relations with the city and state.
- Develop leadership—not just for administrators, but across all groups.
- Improve employee relations and contract management (teachers, paraprofessionals, support staff, and administrators) while designing and negotiating contracts that would facilitate the work that was required (compensation, personal development, career pathways, tuition reimbursement, and meeting and planning time).
- Improve and strengthen city agency collaboration: safety, recreation (after school and summer), finance (tax policy), facilities, and public libraries.
- Improve our public image (and the perception of the district portrayed in the media).

- Build or rehabilitate school buildings.
- Create a sense of urgency.

TRENTON'S ABBOTT IMPLEMENTATION STRATEGY

Ever the optimist, my sense was that if we played our cards right, Abbott could provide an opportunity rather than a problem for us. I also calculated that given the weight of the government actors and advocates behind Abbott, the regulations were going to be implemented whether the urban districts liked them or not, so there was no point in foot-dragging. Although I can't claim that all of the elements of our strategy were developed during a weekend retreat in August 1998, they did take shape as our senior administrative group interacted with the board, our school communities, our employee organizations, and the DOE. To maximize our benefit from Abbott, we took the following approach:

- Submit every plan on or before deadline.
- Be first in line, not last.
- Set out to be the "model" district in Abbott implementation (knowing that the DOE was going to need exemplary districts to prove to the resisters that the timetables and agenda were not unreasonable or undoable).
- Get ahead of the DOE in areas where they were unsure how to proceed (e.g., school-based budgeting, preschool program implementation, facilities planning, and program evaluation design). In other words, create the process and let the DOE learn from us.
- Address DOE areas of concern or dispute (e.g., special education).
- Keep our local elected officials informed, including the mayor, city council, and our legislative delegation (i.e., present an informed and united front in dealing with the DOE).
- Adopt deficit budgets (for fiscal year [FY] 2000 and FY 2001) based on the costs of full implementation of the Abbott provisions, then file appeals with the DOE and courts for full funding (which took courage on the board's part).
- When the DOE offers funding for programs, staffing, and so forth that has not been requested, accept it.
- When dealing with the press, speak of Abbott at all times as an opportunity for Trenton, and don't impugn individuals or support at the DOE.
- Be entrepreneurial. Create new markets (in our case, a hugely successful dropout recovery program) and maintain good relationships

with potential suppliers (e.g., the community-based preschool program providers).

- Form partnerships with major universities, foundations, and government agencies for research projects and experimental programs (i.e., enhance our legitimacy).
- Be proactive, not reactive. Make Trenton a "can do" district. Be nimble and stay ahead of the state, not behind them.

In terms of additional funding, the Trenton strategies proved successful. For both FY 2000 and FY 2001, the Trenton public schools received proportionately more supplemental funding (relative to student enrollment) for whole school reform and for early childhood education and preschool than any city in New Jersey. Per-pupil expenditures increased by $3,000 in two years—to over $15,000 per student—making Trenton at that time among the best funded urban districts in the country. When funding for facilities projects was approved by the legislature, Trenton, following the same first-in-line strategy, again received a higher proportion of its request than any city in New Jersey.

AREAS OF CONTENTION WITH THE DEPARTMENT OF EDUCATION

An obvious problem was that the DOE had been asked to oversee massive organizational change and program implementation when its capacity to lead change was limited. The department was well practiced at developing regulations and ensuring compliance, and at overseeing district-level budget development and audits. But it did not have a theory of "change leadership," particularly for school-level change. Nor was it well attuned to the problems and challenges of urban districts. As a result, the DOE's heavy-handed behavior generated a great deal of resistance and "satisficing" behavior in many of the Abbott districts.

The DOE repeatedly issued regulations and directives without consulting with the urban districts beforehand, and was unwilling to use district-level expertise to provide assistance to other districts. (In Trenton, we took advantage of this situation by developing a consulting business in school-based budgeting, a service we marketed to other Abbott districts.)

A second problem was that the DOE and state administration did not provide funds for Abbott implementation in the department budget for the 1999–2000 (FY 2000) school year, and they grossly underestimated the cost of implementation in the 2000–2001 school year budget. In both years there were controversies between the Abbott districts (such as Trenton) that committed to early implementation and the DOE, because the DOE was unwilling to represent the true cost to the governor and the legislature. Thus, the DOE found itself with binding commitments to the districts and inadequate dollars.

The problem was compounded for FY 2001 because the DOE had developed "illustrative budgets" to assist schools in their budget preparation, and these became *de facto* guarantees for school allocations. But the department had never estimated what the aggregate cost of full implementation would be in the eligible districts, and became aware only late in the process that the cost would be more than triple what had been requested from the legislature. As a result, the department rescinded its original approvals and reduced the amounts it had committed for FY 2001 (in Trenton's case, the reduction was $18 million). Thus, the pressure from the DOE to implement mandated programs was undermined by its underestimates of the costs and resulting litigation brought by the districts.

Another problem was that the DOE was so eager to get national comprehensive school reform providers involved in Abbott that it permitted those it approved to do business without requiring them to address such basic matters as the state's core curriculum content standards or the objectives included in the state assessment program (a situation that was later partially corrected). The DOE also overestimated the capacity of the developers to take on so many schools in such a short period of time (see Lytle, 2002).

Because its salaries were not competitive with those paid by most school districts in the state, and because its senior administrators were appointees who served at the pleasure of the commissioner and the governor, the DOE had continuing problems with employee turnover, further undermining its ability to provide consistent support during implementation.

I could extend this litany of problems, but the basic point is clear. The department did not immediately make a good faith effort to implement Abbott, a matter for which it was heavily criticized by the New Jersey Supreme Court in its March 2000 reaffirmation of the May 1998 opinion. Further, the DOE's capacity to manage a reform effort of the size and complexity of Abbott was suspect from the outset, particularly because it had had no demonstrable success and very public failure in operating the three urban districts it had taken over a decade earlier.

LEADING IN A DYSFUNCTIONAL POLICY ENVIRONMENT

While New Jersey's intervention in its urban districts led to a number of changes in traditional approaches to school district governance and decision making, none of these changes reduced the responsibility of the state's urban superintendents (and their boards) for providing quality education for their students. The leadership challenge for both school boards and superintendents in Abbott districts was complex and fraught with risk.

We were faced with a conundrum: The risk was in complying, and the reward was in complying. Leadership in this context meant:

- Persuading the community that the costs of complying with new state regulations would be outweighed by the benefits, both in additional resources and in learning opportunities for students.
- Pressing principals, teachers, school management teams, and central office staff to get plans and reports done accurately and on time.
- Removing school principals who could not lead reform, and replacing them with ones who could.
- Recruiting a cadre of young minority administrators who would bring a deep sense of moral purpose to their work, as well as strong backgrounds in instructional leadership. (Such individuals could be attracted to Trenton because they would not have to jump all the promotional hurdles large urban districts set up and they could work in a setting where resources were adequate to do the job in a responsible way.)
- Developing contracts (with teacher and administrator employee organizations) that would support reform. (The agreement with Trenton's teachers lengthened instructional time and provided for group planning and conference time during the work day. The agreement with administrators tied the scope of responsibility and degree of accountability to compensation.)
- Persuading teachers and administrators that the comprehensive school reform models were worth trying, while maintaining a degree of skepticism.
- Obtaining and attracting the additional financial and other resources needed to support change.
- Being willing to work with the DOE in supportive ways even when being oppositional in others. (I served on a governor's commission and several DOE task force groups to assist with

policy formation and implementation issues. At the same time, our district sued the DOE four times for not providing funding at the levels we believe Abbott required, and our board twice refused to adopt budgets that did not provide full funding for Abbott implementation, thereby supporting the district's appeals for full funding.)

- Being accessible to the media, and using every opportunity to present the district in a favorable light. (For example, I wrote several op-ed pieces for the city's newspaper of record explaining what we were doing and what our accomplishments were.)

- Taking personal risks. (As an example, I stepped in to serve as interim principal at the high school in the spring of my first year as superintendent when the principal went out on extended sick leave in response to an impending transfer. While at the high school, I had to deal with a student walkout over proposed organizational changes, and with the subsequent media coverage.)

- Understanding the dynamics of disruptive change and, to the degree possible, making them work to the organization's advantage (see Christensen & Overdorf, 2000). When we submitted our initial set of Abbott plans to the DOE, we brought them in a big cardboard box, had the high school band assemble outside the department's front door, and delivered them personally to the assistant secretary of education. Just by coincidence, the media had been invited, and the next day's newspaper ran a feature story with a picture of us handing over the box. We knew the department wasn't expecting the urban school districts to meet its unrealistic deadline, but we were employing "judo strategy," outmaneuvering a larger opponent to gain advantage (see Yoffie & Cusumano, 1999).

- Understanding that reform will only happen if or when a deeper sense of community responsibility and diffused or distributed leadership can be established. (We developed an array of in-district leadership support, coaching, and development programs for administrators, teacher leaders, and school management team chairs.) (See Block, 1997; Elmore, 2000.)

- Becoming a skilled "sensor" (one who collects and interprets soft data), and daring to be different, to capitalize on one's unique characteristics and abilities (see Goffee & Jones, 2000).

- Creating a learning organization, modeling good teaching in one's own work, and keeping teaching and instruction at the front of the organization's priorities or foci (see Elmore, 2000; Wetlaufer, 1999).

- Making inquiry a core process; tying accountability (e.g., performance and descriptive data) to institutional research; teaching administrators and teacher leaders how to use data for formative purposes, with the emphasis on interpreting, redesigning, and changing practice.
- Making school-specific descriptive and performance data public, readily available, and the basis for community engagement in improving schools. (In Trenton's case, the process was facilitated by contracting with IBM to build a "data warehouse.")
- Forming partnerships with major universities, foundations, and government agencies for research projects and experimental programs to enhance our legitimacy in the eyes of our community and the DOE.
- Keeping the moral purpose (see Fullan, 1993) of our reform efforts at the center of all talk about change (which meant, for example, repeatedly expressing concern about high dropout rates, special education referrals and enrollments, suspension rates, and course failure rates at all grade levels). We regularly monitored and discussed data related to these issues. I also made it a point to be informed on national research on each issue.

The concept of disruptive change could bear some amplification. The term was coined by Christensen and Overdorf (2000) in a *Harvard Business Review* article. Successful companies, they argue, "are pretty good at responding to evolutionary changes in their markets . . . [or] *sustaining innovation.* Where they run into trouble is in handling or initiating revolutionary changes in their markets, or dealing with *disruptive innovation*" (p. 71). For Trenton, the disruptive innovation had been charter schools. The school board had strenuously opposed them, but the state DOE had consistently overruled the board and supported charter school creation. The district had groused about the charter schools, but had not come up with a way to redesign its own schools and programs to counter their impact. (That was about to change.)

Many of the Abbott districts, and to some extent the state DOE, had great difficulty in managing the disruptive change that the Abbott decree forced. Trenton, on the other hand, was able to take advantage of the Abbott mandates (and funding) to strengthen itself as an organization. By aggressively expanding preschool services, lengthening the school day in elementary schools, increasing access to technology, reducing class size, improving instructional program quality, redesigning the high school, and opening a dropout re-entry school, we were able to increase enrollment by 25 percent within a three-year period—while the city's charter schools rapidly lost enrollment.

MAKING THE LEAP

We had formulated the approach we would take to the challenge of making Abbott the lever for change in Trenton. In outlining the strategies we pursued, I have previewed some results that were achieved. But outlines can't begin to describe the difficulty and complexity of the work—or the leadership that would be required. In the chapters that follow, I will illustrate in greater detail just what systemic reform would mean for Trenton.

7

Designing and Getting Under Way

Earlier I listed the extensive set of challenges that had become apparent during my entry as Trenton's superintendent. In retrospect, I can see that there were four overlapping areas we needed to address quickly. The first was structural—designing our budget development process, our teacher contract, and our data management systems so that they would support rather than hinder our reform efforts. Simultaneously, we needed to improve our instructional programs by implementing the comprehensive school reform programs the Court and Department of Education (DOE) had mandated. We were also aware that the depth and breadth of the reforms we were undertaking would require leadership at every level, from the Board of Education through to the classroom, so we needed to institute an array of leadership development initiatives. Finally, we were aware of our obligation to show that these reforms were making a demonstrable and significant difference for our students; that meant we had to have suitable monitoring and accountability systems in place.

In this context, my leadership would be measured by my ability to ensure that we had designed and implemented the necessary policies, practices, and operating systems. Then I and our senior leadership team needed to be able to teach our employees and the community how to operate in these new conditions. And we needed to demonstrate that we were being good stewards, both in respect to improving our services to our students and in terms of how we were using newly available resources to achieve our goals.

WORKING TO BECOME A LEARNING-TO-LEARN ORGANIZATION

The notion of learning organization has been central to the organizational reform and redesign literature for at least the past two decades (e.g., Senge, 1990). Because schools and school districts are supposed to be organizations whose first purpose is to help their students learn, it would seem obvious that they should themselves be learning organizations and that their employees should experience them in that way. As one familiar with the literature on learning organizations, and one who has tried to create these sorts of organizations in whatever leadership role I have held, I came to Trenton with the intent of making us a learning and learning-to-learn district.

As I described in chapter 6, I began my service in Trenton by conducting a series of public "fishbowl" meetings with division heads for the various components of the district (e.g., federal programs, transportation, maintenance). The district budget had been adopted several months before my arrival, and one objective for me was getting the division heads to explain their budgets. District employees and the general public were invited to attend—and to participate by asking questions and making recommendations after the initial presentation—and the meetings were televised on our public access channel.

Although audiences shifted from meeting to meeting, over the two-week period they included city council members, school board members, employee organization officers, parent and community organization leaders, interested employees, and members of the general public. In addition to providing the district contextual information I needed, the meetings gave me an opportunity to quickly establish new norms for the district and the community. All budget information was public. All monies belonged to the schools, the students, and the parents (and none for perpetuating fiefdoms). And I had an opportunity not only to establish myself as knowledgeable about budgets and operations, areas my predecessors had kept a distance from, but also to present myself as the district's "lead teacher" (see Tichy, 2002).

STRUCTURAL CHANGE

Participatory and Opportunity-to-Learn Processes

The process of open critique exemplified in the fishbowl meetings quickly translated into a school-based budget development process during fall 1998. Abbott regulations required that school budgets be developed by each school management team (SMT) and that as great a proportion as possible of district funds be allocated to schools (in Trenton's case, this meant about 60 percent). We gave every principal a laptop with a spreadsheet already installed, taught principals and SMT members how to use the spreadsheet and how to develop a budget to meet state expectations, and succeeded in meeting a very tight deadline. The ancillary benefit was that principals, teachers, parents, and our employee organizations emerged from the process with a much greater understanding of costs, priority setting, and resource utilization than they had had before the process began.

The budget development process is only one of many ways in which we worked to create a learning-to-learn organization. In my second year, I used two-thirds of the biweekly principals' meeting time to teach a course in organizational theory so that we might move toward a shared understanding of schools as organizations. We also committed to making descriptive and performance data for our schools public by developing detailed school profiles that would be available to teachers, parents, and the community in booklet form and on our website. A new IBM "data warehouse" (described in more detail later in this chapter) made report generation timely and easy for those interested, and it tied our state-mandated accountability planning and quality assurance reporting to our database. The intent was to facilitate the ready access to data that would allow us to concentrate on formative evaluation and quality improvement over the next several years. By having schools present their performance objectives, performance histories, and improvement plans to the board at its monthly meetings, we were able to educate the board so that we could focus on long-term, continuous instructional improvement rather than on short-term problems.

Designing Employee Organization Contracts as Levers for Learning

In each of our employee contract negotiations, whether with professional or classified employees, we sought to encourage continuous learning by including tuition benefits for further education. As one example, we provided tuition benefits at the local state college rate for all paraprofessionals. We also sought to encourage career opportunities for the paraprofessionals by offering release time for those who needed to do student teaching as part of a teacher training program. To encourage administrators to get further education and training, we agreed that they could attend any educational leadership program they chose without regard to tuition cost.

Teacher Contract Negotiations in Trenton

Our contract negotiation with the teachers' association provides the clearest illustration of how we designed agreements that demonstrated our commitment to being a learning-to-learn organization.

As I have previously suggested, in my first year as superintendent in Trenton I was making good progress in gaining support from the community, the political sector, the state DOE, and the board. I had also worked to change the relationship between principals and the superintendent by designing and conducting biweekly administrative meetings in ways that were intended to teach and build capacity. My relationship with the teachers' union was open—mostly respectful and occasionally contentious (for example, when an employee grievance was brought to me for resolution). The contract with the teachers was due to expire in the summer of my second year, and I knew that we were going to have to make substantial changes in contract language if we were to have any hope of improving student achievement on a long-term, consistent basis.

With the board's concurrence, I proposed that the two negotiating teams participate in a summer retreat at an off-site conference center to develop a framework for conducting negotiations. I suggested that a facilitator acceptable to both parties design and conduct the retreat, and consult with both parties on creating the agenda. The union agreed to consider the plan, and I contacted Pat Sanaghan, a consultant I had worked with in Philadelphia who had once been a special education teacher. We set the date, and he moved back and forth between the parties, finally getting consent on an agenda for the two days. The administration team included the board president and another board member, the superintendent (me), and senior administrators. The union's team included officers representing a cross-section of the district's schools, as well as a state union advisor. By mutual agreement, neither team included an attorney; we were not going to negotiate, only get to know each other.

We arrived at the hotel in mid-morning and gathered for our first session. The union immediately announced that they were not comfortable with the agenda and were going to leave if we insisted on sticking to it. Fortunately, Sanaghan, the facilitator, was skilled enough to deal with the anxiety and resistance, and he began to work with the union leadership to examine the reasons for their oppositional stance. He gradually determined that they felt that the board members and administrators, including the new superintendent, were not respectful or aware of the union's history in dealing with the district. So he suggested that we all create a "history wall" with four decades as the intervals. We would each write our personal and work histories on sticky notes, then stick them in the appropriate decade.

The collective histories were a revelation. As an example, the teachers' notes spoke of a bitter relationship with the district in the early and mid-1980s, when none of the current board members or administrators was in the district. For three successive years the teachers had worked without pay raises, and in each year there were massive layoffs in June followed by rehirings in August. In lieu of pay increases, the board had added sick days to teachers' leave banks, but those were of no immediate value. For the teachers, their contract symbolized the years of contentiousness, poor treatment, and sacrifice.

The administrators and board members listened intently as the teachers told story after story about how they had experienced this period in the district, and why it had led to long-standing suspicion and anger. Because we were willing to listen, be empathetic, and learn, the level of trust between the two groups changed for the better. The retreat ended with a shared commitment to reach an early settlement.

By the following March, five months before the contract expiration date, we had concluded negotiations and ratified an agreement—lengthening the instructional day and the school year, providing more time for teachers to talk with each other, reducing the number of steps on the salary scale, and creating new teacher leader positions with increased pay for increased responsibilities. There had never before been an early settlement, and the union membership was jubilant. In the process we had changed the relationship between teachers and administration, acknowledging that the teachers had primary responsibility for student learning, and that the administration's job was to help teachers do their work as effectively as possible. We had acknowledged our mutual dependency.

Ultimately, this story is about leadership for learning. But its complexity suggests how the parties—the board, administration, teachers' union leadership, and state association leadership—needed to work over a period of time to understand each other's needs and concerns before they could move to an agreement. This "adaptive" work preceded the technical work—the salary tables and contract language that embodied the terms of the agreement. This is also a story about educational reform, and about how policy documents such as teacher contracts have direct bearing on the conditions that make effective schooling possible. Sustainable reform requires this sort of deep structural work. Finally, it is a story about the satisfactions of leadership and illustrates how leadership can sometimes mean being a participant in the process, not simply leading the process.

System-Level Information Management:
Building a Data Warehouse

Another "design and build" challenge was to rapidly increase the district's capacity for information and data management. When I arrived at Trenton, one of the problems I soon encountered was that many of the divisions maintained separate computer-based records and operating systems, including student records (attendance, standardized test scores, report cards, high school schedules, transcripts, etc.), special education, transportation, food services, security, business (school and district budgets, purchasing, payroll), personnel and human resources, and Board of Education records.

In Trenton, each division had designed its system to serve its own needs, and each was leery of combining its records with those other divisions lest "important" information get lost. At another level, each was aware that information is a source of power, and that control of information gives one power. That was one reason why sharing data across divisions, making data accessible and public, was a potential source of conflict. Yet I was well aware of the high cost of maintaining all these separate data systems, both in terms of personnel time and equipment and in terms of the organization's capacity to understand itself and monitor its performance.

I also recognized the advantages of a well-designed information system. Imagine, for example, that the state DOE wants to know how many high school students are being taught by appropriately certified teachers (i.e., math courses by math-certified teachers). Answering that question requires working across at least two data sets, student records and personnel, and perhaps even special education. Without an integrated data system, responding to such questions can be time consuming and laborious. The leadership challenge in Trenton was to continually press for transparency and collaboration in system design and use, recognizing that this was not simply addressing the technical problem of building an integrated data system, but rather the much larger goal of building a collaborative working environment and norms of trust and public accountability.

The solution to our situation was to build a data warehouse that would function as a repository for the many different data sets the district maintained. In theory, a data warehouse supports connections across each division's data sets and file systems without having to reformat or re-enter data, even if the files have been developed and maintained using distinct software packages from different vendors. We issued a request for proposals, selected IBM as our vendor, and worked with them to build a high-functioning warehouse.

An immediate advantage of the new data warehouse was that it would allow us to develop school profiles modeled on the ones I had designed and published in Philadelphia. Trenton had never made school demographic and performance data public, and I was determined that the entire school district community should have access to school-specific data. We developed statistical descriptions, or profiles, for each school in the district, including everything from student demographics to teacher qualifications to test scores and promotion and retention data. The profiles were made available to teachers, parents, and the community in booklet form and on the district website.

The profiles included no evaluative component. Instead, users could look at data for their own schools and for comparable schools, then draw their own conclusions. The intent was to support community inquiry, to make information about our schools transparent, and to create a sense of collective responsibility for improving performance. This was another example of system design to support teaching and learning and demonstrate our stewardship.

STRENGTHENING INSTRUCTION

Comprehensive School Reform as Capital Acquisition

As outlined in chapter 6, one component of the Abbott consent decree was the requirement that all urban schools adopt "research-based," comprehensive school reform models. Elementary schools could choose among eight approved models or could accept the default model (Success for All). Although the demographics of Trenton's elementary schools were roughly similar, their performance histories differed markedly. Some had been high-performing for years, and others were consistently low-performing.

In conversations with principals and central office administrators, it became apparent that there was no single reform model that would be appropriate for every school. Some models stressed early-grade basic skills, others focused on school climate, and others required careful alignment of the school's curriculum and assessment programs. None had an established research base indicating that it was demonstrably better than the others. In the spirit of becoming a learning-to-learn organization, we decided that the most sensible approach for us as a district administration was to help the schools make informed choices from the menu of models. The central office provided SMTs with detailed information on each model, and coordinated discussions with the model providers. We wanted to be sure that, in the face of a state-mandated reform program, schools felt they had some degree of choice in determining how they would go about improving their own programs.

There was another benefit to implementing comprehensive school reform models. I had come to Trenton with intellectual and social capital developed over the course of my career, but the knowledge and the contacts were embedded within me and were meaningful only if I could use them to build organizational capital and leverage for the district. That required that I act as a bridge between individuals and organizations that could increase the district's capital. I was well aware of the design problems and limitations of the various models, but, as I wrote in a *Phi Delta Kappan* article:

> For us the benefits of being involved in whole-school reform extend well beyond learning and implementing the model. For the first time our teachers and principals are engaged in national and regional networks of practitioners with whom they share many more interests and concerns than just their experience with the model. Their conversations with colleagues from across the country have helped them become less parochial and more open to change.
>
> Through implementing the comprehensive school reform models we have become much more focused on student performance and evidence as we plan the work of school and much more focused on curriculum, teaching, and learning as we carry out that work. Our teachers have accepted leadership roles in improving instruction, in part because most of the models require teacher facilitators who provide collegial coaching and support. Faculties are developing a sense of collective responsibility for student performance. We are doing better at involving parents and teachers in school decision making. And we are learning to make good use of consultants and resource people as we move from reform to continuous improvement. (Lytle, 2002, p. 165)

We were using the comprehensive school reform implementation process to build organizational, social, and intellectual capital. And we added a strategic twist. The model developers were all part of a consortium, New American Schools Development Corporation (NASDC), which acted as a conduit for federal research and development funding. We negotiated a contract with NASDC to help us with implementation and serve as an intermediary with the model developers. But an additional reason for the contract was to provide us an alternate route to the developers, reducing our dependence on the state DOE and increasing our legitimacy as a reform district.

Increasing Market Share

When I came to Trenton, the district's enrollment had been dropping sharply as charter schools competed for students. We conducted market research to understand why we had lost so many students, and one of the things we learned was that the charter schools offered child care before and after school. This was a situation we could address quickly by adding before-school and after-school programs in our elementary schools. Thus, our children could be at school from 7:30 a.m. to 5:00 or 5:30 p.m., and we had canceled out one key recruiting feature of the charter schools.

To provide an incentive for kids to come early, we instituted federally subsidized breakfast programs in all of our elementary schools. This allowed us to staff the before-school programs with the cost being borne by food services. Another component of the response was to work closely with the city's community-based preschool program providers. As they expanded programs for three- and four-year-olds, we looked to them as "feeders" for our kindergarten programs. Within a year, our elementary school enrollments began to climb.

Our most successful move was to develop a whole new market. At my instigation, we established a dropout recovery program in a leased parochial school facility and recruited potential students from street corners, barbershops, and beauty parlors across the city. The results exceeded our greatest hopes: More than one thousand students were enrolled in the program at some point during its first year, and 287 of those met high school graduation requirements, more than doubling the number of graduates from the previous year. (A more complete version of the Trenton Daylight/Twilight story is included in chapter 10.)

LEADERSHIP DEVELOPMENT

The Right People On the Bus

In *Good to Great*, Jim Collins (2001) talks about the importance of getting the right people on the bus if an organization is going to have any real prospect for improving performance for the long term. To get the district moving in the right direction, we needed to add seasoned people who knew New Jersey, knew the state DOE, knew urban schools, knew their own territory—and were not imbued with Trenton's defeatist culture. They had to be instantly credible, and they had to be able to lead and manage without oversight from me. They needed to be strong, technically proficient, and independent. Most important, they had to be committed to improving circumstances and opportunity for urban, poor, minority students. Over the course of my first two years, I recruited what I considered an all-star team. Some were appointed in positions I created, others in vacancies created when those who weren't comfortable with the pace of reform chose to exit. In order of their appointments, these individuals included:

- Paul Kadri, a graduate student of mine while he was getting his MBA at the University of Pennsylvania. Paul had worked at IBM, and then as an aide to the mayor of Jersey City and an assistant to a regional superintendent in Newark. He had strengths in finance and technology, areas where we needed expertise. Paul served as an assistant superintendent overseeing the implementation of our computer network and our school-based budget system.
- Mel Wyns, budget director for the DOE. He was recognized as someone with unimpeachable integrity and as the most knowledgeable person in the state regarding state education finance policy and operations. He had grown tired of the machinations in the department and of being passed over for promotion to assistant commissioner. When I asked him to consider becoming our business administrator, the chance to take a senior position in an Abbott district near his home was irresistible. His appointment gave us immediate leverage and credibility with the DOE, and ultimately it meant millions of dollars in additional revenue for the district because of his understanding of how the state allocation process worked.
- Dave Kelter, in charge of scheduling at University City High School and a key partner in our high school reform consulting company. Because scheduling is so often the barrier in school reform efforts, I knew that Dave would be a key resource for the reform work in Trenton. I also knew that Dave was an expert on efficient staff utilization; when we wanted or needed to capture the dollar and human resource inefficiencies in schools, Dave would be invaluable.
- Priscilla Dawson, an elementary and middle school principal in Philadelphia, and Principal of the Year in honor of her work at Gillespie Middle School (and she had taken a course from me at Penn). Although I had encouraged her to apply for the Trenton Central High School principalship, she was selected for the position by the SMT (following the forced departure of the long-time incumbent). She brought a high degree of professionalism and commitment to create a high-expectations, caring school environment.
- Bill Tracy, a teacher leader at University City High School, whose effectiveness with resistant and rebellious students was

the reason I encouraged him to apply for the principalship of the Daylight/Twilight School. Bill had resisted becoming a school administrator, perhaps because his father had been his high school principal. But I was confident that he could make our new school work.

- Gloria Hancock, chief of staff for the New Jersey DOE. She was intimately familiar with the workings of the department and with state regulation. More importantly, she wanted an opportunity to work more closely with urban minority children. Gloria accepted a position as assistant superintendent for student services, an area needing aggressive oversight and increased connection to city agencies and the community.

The Right People Off the Bus: Gracious Exits

As my understanding of individual schools and central office support services deepened during my first year, it became clear that there were a number of principals and central office administrators who weren't able or willing to undertake the reform agenda the state, the mayor, the board, and I had set for the district. We needed to get some folks off the bus so we could get some others on.

One step I took to address this situation was to persuade the board to offer a one-time retirement incentive package to our administrators. With the board's approval, we offered to pay the full value of all accumulated leave, including vacation, personal leave, and sick days, to anyone agreeing to retire by June 30. For many older administrators, that meant the equivalent of a year or more of salary in addition to their retirement benefits. To make the package cost-neutral, I proposed to eliminate a number of central office positions (such as curriculum supervisor), knowing that the additional funding we were receiving from Abbott would allow us to replace these supports with teacher leaders at the school level. The retirement incentive plan worked as we had intended, providing a respectful and gracious exit plan for many of our old-timers, streamlining the central office, and creating school-based leadership vacancies for both administrators and teachers—making possible the recruitment and appointment of next-generation leaders.

The Right People Off the Bus: Zero Tolerance

In *Managing the Unexpected*, Karl Weick and Kathleen Sutcliffe (2001) make the case that it is how leaders deal with unanticipated events that most directly communicates their values and builds trust.

I had been superintendent in Trenton for just over a year when the director of student services came into my office to tell me that the mother of an eighth grade student had come to see him about transferring her daughter from one of our middle schools to another. As she discussed the reasons for her request, he learned that the girl had been signed out of school by an "uncle" several times the previous spring and taken to his house for sex. The mother had contacted the school principal to find out how this could have happened without her knowledge. According to her, the principal had belittled her and called her daughter a slut. Although the mother was angry about her treatment by the principal and concerned about her daughter, she decided not to file a complaint, but instead just wanted to get her daughter on a safe track at another school.

Both the director and I were aware that the principal had a legally binding requirement to immediately report even the suspicion of sexual abuse to the state department of child protective services. That had not been done. I asked the director to visit the school and examine the available records, including the early dismissal forms. His investigation revealed that the discipline dean had permitted the man to sign the girl out four times between February and May, and that the dean had made no attempt to contact the girl's mother to determine whether the dismissals were being made with her consent. The principal provided a report of police department contact regarding the matter, but the police denied knowledge of the contact. There was no record that the state department of child services had been contacted until September, after our investigation had begun.

The principal was an African American male who lived in the community where the school was located. Although considered a "character," he had a reputation for running a tight school and for being a political activist. He had been a resistant participant in our principals' meetings and was unenthusiastic about proposed reforms. When I began a formal investigation and hearing process, he took the position that his judgment was in keeping with community standards, that I was out to get him, and that I was out of order in suggesting he had acted inappropriately. Meanwhile, the police had arrested the "uncle," and within months he was in prison. I filed tenure charges recommending the principal's dismissal for cause. All through the investigation I kept the board president and mayor informed. They supported my position, although they took considerable heat from some of their constituents.

Given the extraordinarily convoluted processes that dismissal requires in New Jersey, the board, on the advice of their attorney, agreed to the principal's resignation. In my judgment, there had been no room for compromise about his departure. Parents have the right to expect that their children will be safe in our keeping. District employees have an absolute responsibility to protect children.

The Prospective Hazards of Administrator Departure

This story illustrates an important leadership skill—the ability to be a good "situation sensor," able to "collect and interpret soft data[,] . . . sniff out the signals in the environment[,] and sense what's going on without having anything spelled out" (Goffee & Jones, 2000, p. 66). As a new white superintendent pushing for the dismissal of an iconic black principal, I needed to understand and manage the context in which I was operating. Being right would not have been sufficient.

During my first year I removed two other principals—both also African American—from their schools. In one of these cases, I decided to "non-renew" the contract of an elementary principal we had hired just before the opening of school. Although she had a doctorate and good technical skills, her relationships with teachers and parents had been contentious, and she had shown no willingness to change her ways. The other individual was a senior high school principal who had acknowledged that he couldn't provide the kind of leadership that redesigning and reforming the high school would require, and he agreed to be reassigned to a central office vacancy. Then he went out on extended sick leave, and I ended up serving as interim principal in his school for the remainder of the school year.

The combination of the three forced departures (along with the retirement incentive program) prompted an underground campaign against me for racial profiling, which naturally led to a number of newspaper stories. I had kept the mayor and the board informed at every step, and I knew from my sensing activity that support for each of the three individuals was thin. Within a month of their removals, the board president (himself African American) told me that everywhere he went he was getting positive support for these "firings." A common perception, he said, was that the district must finally be serious about reform and about making things better because we were getting rid of people who everyone knew should have been gone long ago. The board president and I both understood that being good stewards required ensuring that the district's leaders embody its values and willingly undertake its work.

Building a Bench: Next-Generation Leadership

Getting the right people on and off the bus may be necessary, but it is certainly not sufficient. For the long term, we needed to build leadership capacity throughout the organization, particularly at the principal and teacher levels. I also needed to be sure that there were several people in the district who would be ready to replace me when the time for my departure came. During the 2004–2005 school year, my seventh as superintendent, I recommended two of our outstanding principals for promotion to assistant superintendent positions and recruited a third person from the state DOE who was also appointed an assistant superintendent. Their appointments solidified our increasing focus on instructional improvement, but also put them in position to demonstrate their suitability as prospective superintendents.

Chapter 9 expands on this important issue—how we made leadership development the center of our strategic planning and development.

ACCOUNTABILITY

Testing Our Students: Whose Test Counts?

The measure of success for Trenton's schools and students, and for the district, had historically been the state-mandated testing program administered in grades 3, 8, and 11 (later expanded to grades 3–8 to meet the requirements of the No Child Left Behind Act). The problems with the state program were threefold:

- The publishers would not provide technical manuals, so test interpretation was difficult.
- The state testing office repeatedly changed its standards for proficiency, making year-to-year comparisons questionable.
- There were different test publishers for each of the three grades, making it impossible to measure growth over time.

Our response was to administer a nationally-normed and widely used achievement test, *Terra Nova* (published by CTB/McGraw-Hill). That allowed us to include *Terra Nova* results in our school profiles and have a reliable way to track individual student performance from year to year, something the state testing program could not do. In deciding to conduct our own testing program, we had made a strategic move. Rather than let the state be the sole determiner of our performance, we intentionally put in place a widely used test that would allow us to demonstrate our accomplishments (and shortcomings) in a more valid and reliable way than the state's program did. In so doing, we were demonstrating our willingness to be more accountable than the state required, and in the process we were increasing our credibility.

Program Evaluation through Cohort Tracking Studies

I have been making the case throughout this book that leadership requires knowing what matters to whom, and being able to anticipate questions and shape public discourse. In the realm of academic accountability, that may well require investing in long-term research and evaluation projects, where the payoff can be years away. This premise is well illustrated by a comparison between the approaches to evaluating preschool programs in Philadelphia and in New Jersey.

When I was research director in Philadelphia, one of the studies we were conducting got consistent national attention—researching the long-term effects of preschool. The study began as an evaluation of our Follow Through program, a preschool program for three- and four-year-olds from low-income families. Students were tracked for fifteen years (or longer), until they finished high school. Each year, a variety of indicators were observed for all students in each Follow Through cohort and recorded in the district's data warehouse. Interim reports were generated and provided to program directors, the superintendent, and early childhood educators. The emergent findings were compelling, and they influenced national policy on preschool. Participating children were less likely to drop out, more likely to complete high school, less likely to be referred to special education, less likely to be retained in grade, more likely to have good report card grades, and less likely to have discipline problems—a substantial return on the investment.

My experience in Trenton provides a counterexample. An important provision of the Abbott mandate was that preschool programs be initiated for all three- and four-year-olds living in the state's thirty poorest cities, but the state DOE made no effort to evaluate the programs. Given the cost of the programs, and the concerns of the state legislature about the new expenditure, I considered it grossly irresponsible that the DOE wasn't willing to work with the thirty districts to design and conduct a long-term tracking study to answer questions about the benefits of the investment and to guide program improvement. (In Trenton we were able to do a primitive version of a tracking study for preschool program participants, which suggested that the benefits were similar to those seen in Philadelphia.)

The benefits of tracking studies apply equally at the school level. As a principal, I was never willing to let the central office unilaterally determine the criteria for success, and I made it a practice to conduct tracking studies of our school's graduates, whether eighth graders going on to high school or twelfth graders going on to college or work. By following up on our graduates, we were able to determine what they were doing and how prepared they felt they were for the next level, allowing us to make program adjustments. In addition, the data from this sort of evaluation can make a compelling case for continuing support and investment in a program. For example, Daylight/Twilight, the Trenton dropout recovery school (which is described in detail in chapter 10), could present persuasive data demonstrating that 85 to 90 percent of its graduates were working, in college, or in the armed services. (Doing this sort of study can be simple and fun. Teachers are invited to stay at school one evening to call a list of graduates [for a large class, a sample is sufficient]. If the graduate is home, then he or she is interviewed; if not, a parent or sibling can act as informant. Usually the graduate or family is thrilled to be called by someone from their former school, and they make wonderful sources of data.)

A FIRM FOUNDATION

The first stage of building a robust learning community in Trenton was well under way. Structural changes were strengthening the district's ability to support reform, the implementation of the Abbott mandates (while cumbersome at times) was providing resources and impetus for significant improvement in instructional programs, key staffing changes and leadership development activities were strengthening the human resources of the district, and we were increasing transparency and accountability (in terms of both student achievement and our responsibility to the community).

Now we were ready to build on this foundation of intellectual, social, and organizational capital to open up new opportunities for our students and strengthen our community.

8

Building Capacity

Building Trenton's organizational capacity proceeded on many fronts. We made leadership development our first priority, but we also undertook a number of other systemic changes, including the second-stage work on school improvement and curriculum reform, along with a massive school construction program. Collectively, the stories in this chapter illustrate how and why we were evolving as a more effective and successful organization.

BUILDING LEADERSHIP

When the No Child Left Behind Act was enacted in 2001, it established a national goal of 100 percent of students reaching proficiency in reading and mathematics by the year 2014, yet still no one claims to know how to attain that goal. Although states maintain that more and more of their grade 3–12 students are meeting proficiency standards, SAT verbal and mathematics scores have shown virtually no improvement for the last two decades, and American students do not compare favorably with students from other first world countries on international tests of science and mathematics. The corporate sector has consistently outpaced the education sector in invention and innovation. So how can school leaders take some lessons from the business world and go about creating the conditions for continuous learning and continuous improvement? For working toward ambitious goals? For knowledge generation?

A compelling answer comes from the Toyota Corporation, which makes organizational learning the core of its business model. The company "views employees not just as pairs of hands but as knowledge workers who accumulate *chie*—the wisdom of experience—on the company's front lines. Toyota therefore invests heavily in people and organizational capabilities, and it garners ideas from everywhere: the shop floor, the office, the field" (Takeuchi, Osono, & Shimizu, 2008, p. 98). The company also values the "tacit knowledge rooted in each employee's actions and experiences" (p. 102). Contemplating such a model in an educational context raises at least two big questions: How many districts, states, and universities view school teachers as knowledge workers? And what would it mean for schools and school districts to operate as true learning organizations?

Developing a "Leaderful" Community in Trenton

Trenton makes an interesting case study in leadership because it was the recipient of two major national leadership development grants—a Leadership for Educational Achievement in Districts (LEAD) grant from Wallace/Reader's Digest Funds, and a U.S. Department of Education School Leadership Program grant. The Trenton case illustrates an approach to long-term organizational improvement that is very different from the norm in education, and shows how the locus for leadership development is moving away from college and university educational administration programs and toward district-generated and district-controlled programs—in the manner of Toyota.

In 2000 and 2001, a series of small grants (totaling more than $100,000) permitted the district to begin working with organizational development consultants on leading change. Based in large part on the success of this preliminary work, Trenton was one of twelve urban districts awarded a LEAD grant. The grant made Trenton part of a national network of states, cities, universities, and research and development organizations working to tie educational leadership more closely to classrooms and student performance.

The five-year, $5 million LEAD grant, in combination with a three-year School Leadership Program grant and funds the district committed, meant that Trenton was able to underwrite leadership development from the level of the board through to paraprofessionals and student government. The expectation was that by making the district a community of leaders—a "leaderful" community—the likelihood of sustainable improvement could be maximized.

Table 8.1 provides a list and very brief description of the array of leadership programs and strategies implemented in the district. As the table illustrates, colleges and universities played a limited role in

Trenton's leadership development efforts. Rather, Trenton took what might be considered an entrepreneurial and corporate approach, using its discretionary funds to contract with consultants whose experience and expertise exceeded that of area university faculty members.

The overarching framework for making Trenton a leadership learning community drew heavily on corporate leadership development strategies, particularly at General Electric (see Tichy, 2002), where CEO Jack Welch considered teaching as his most important role. The district's leadership development design team was also influenced by the work of Collins (2001), Heifetz, and Linsky (Heifetz, 1994; Heifetz & Linsky, 2002) because of their ability to relate leadership behavior so directly to organizational performance. Collins helped us understand the conditions that characterize successful organizations. Heifetz and Linsky provided insights into the challenges, satisfactions, and dangers of leadership.

Trenton's Leadership Challenge

Because we were in the midst of so much organizational change, and because effective leadership relates directly to improved student performance, we determined that leadership development should be the center of the district's strategic plan. Our building-level leadership was stable enough that we didn't need to worry about recruiting new principals, so we could use grant funds to connect leadership and organizational development in ways that made the two symbiotic. That approach included the board and superintendent, central office and school administrators, teacher leaders, employee association leaders, and parent and student leadership.

The primary challenge in Trenton was to move from a state-mandated instructional improvement process, centered on comprehensive school reform, to a more adaptive approach to improving student achievement, and to deal with implementation overload caused by the state's shotgun approach to urban school reform.

Historically, the district had operated as a highly centralized organization. Various central offices provided oversight and direction for all schools, and principals were expected to be "operational champions," implementing policies and programs dictated by higher administration. When the state undertook its urban school reform initiative in fall 1998, it adopted an approach that reinforced the principals' pattern of dependency, substituting its strategies for those that had previously been mandated by the central office. (See Lytle, 2002, for a fuller discussion of the whole school reform process, which is also discussed in

Table 8.1. Trenton as a Leadership Learning Community

Participating Groups: Board of Education, superintendent and senior administration, principals and vice principals, central office administrative support staff, teacher leaders, union and support staff leadership, student leaders

Theory of Action: Having an array of leadership development programs and job opportunities that are intentionally managed by senior leadership acting as designers, mentors, and steerspersons

Student Involvement: Participation in a wide variety of leadership activities, ranging from student government to peer mentoring and representation on the Board of Education

Job-Embedded Activities:
- *Policy governance:* The board leading for improved student performance (The Aspen Group)
- *Comprehensive school reform developer meetings:* Both regional and national
- *State professional organizations:* For example, New Jersey Principals and Supervisors Association
- *Evidence-based leadership:* Facilitated by use of the new student data management system (SASI)
- *Monthly administrative roundtable meetings:* Planned by the participants
- *Executive coaching:* Available as needed for new administrators and others as may be required
- *Teacher networks:* Teacher-generated and led; function in lieu of a curriculum office
- *Teacher leadership positions:* Whole school reform and technology facilitators, small learning community teacher leaders ($N = 110+$)

Developmental Activities:

- **Ventures in Leadership seminars:** Intrapersonal, interpersonal, and systemic leadership (Sanaghan Associates)
- **Leadership Trenton:** Local leadership development program crossing many organizations, both profit and nonprofit
- **US Department of Education School Leadership Program:** For new and prospective administrators (with two other New Jersey cities: Newark and Patterson) (Center for Evidence-Based Education [CEBE])
- **Tuition reimbursement for graduate work:** For example, administrative certification, doctoral study

Combination of Job-Embedded and Developmental Activities:

- **School Inquiry/School Review:** A three-year, school-specific, collegial, in-depth instructional program critique (with an ancillary instructional leadership development dimension) (CEBE)

Goals:

- Develop social, intellectual, and organizational capital (see Hargreaves, 1997)
- Improve organizational performance in relation to the board's goals
- Learn across boundaries

- **Principal certification program and related research and mentoring programs:** Collaborative relationship with The College of New Jersey
- **Leadership for Educational Achievement in Districts superintendents seminar:** Conducted at Kennedy School of Government, Center for Public Leadership, Harvard University
- **Career ladders:** Teacher leaders, vice principals, and assistant directors
- **International study visits and Carpe Vitam:** A seven-nation, school-based project on school reform underwritten by the Wallenburg Foundation; principals, board members, senior administrators

- Increase/develop networks and connectivity
- Create classroom-level critical discourse
- Learn our way to new levels of performance
- Institutionalize leadership development so that it is a continuing practice and investment

chapter 7.) As a result, the definition of successful school leadership continued to be "doing as one was told," but it was the state, not the district, that was doing the telling.

In *Leadership without Easy Answers*, Ron Heifetz warns of the limits of this top-down, prescriptive approach to leadership, then talks about the unique kinds of leadership that are required when one is dealing with complex problems for which "no adequate response has yet been developed" (1994, p. 72). Certainly such challenges as educational equity for urban, minority, poor students and reducing the achievement gap fall into that category. Heifetz goes on to argue that "seeking solutions from people in authority is maladaptive . . . because it disables some of our most important personal and collective resources for accomplishing adaptive work" (p. 74). Adaptive work is necessary when "[t]he problem definition is not clear-cut and technical fixes are not available. The situation calls for leadership that induces learning. . . . [L]earning is required both to define problems and implement solutions" (p. 75). There were no easy answers to the challenges we were facing in Trenton, our decisions could have life-long impact on our students, and we had to mobilize every possible resource. That is why we chose an adaptive, problem-defining, inquiry approach to leadership development (see also Copland, 2003; Murphy & Datnow, 2003).

Strategic Inquiry

The centerpiece of our leadership development efforts was our strategic inquiry initiative. The Wallace Foundation leadership grant provided funding for a contract with the Center for Evidence-Based Education, whose head, David Green, had been chief inspector in the Inner-London Education Authority before moving to the United States. As an inspector he had spent a great deal of time visiting and evaluating schools, and giving actionable feedback to their head teachers and faculties. Green had become aware of the limitations of that process, particularly the fact that most of the "meaning making" from the inspections was done by the inspectors themselves, not by the school heads and teachers whose behavior and expectations would need to change if their schools were going to do a better job.

Green's work in Trenton gave him and us the opportunity to take the inspection model farther. Under his leadership we designed a process that used teams of principals, teachers, and administrators from the central office to do the "inspecting." A typical team might have ten members and a consultant from Green's organization. The process began with an orientation and training session for the team, as well as an orientation for the school or office that was to be inspected. Then the team spent a week at the school observing every classroom at least once; interviewing teachers, students, and parents; attending school functions; observing in the lunchroom, school yard, and main office; and reviewing student work and school data.

After each day's observations, the team met to discuss their experience and share information. The accumulated data and observations were organized into a twenty- to thirty-page report drafted by week's end. Contents included an assessment of the quality of teaching across all classrooms, with examples of good and poor lessons, as well as more general comments on the overall climate of the school. On Friday afternoon, the team conducted an informal debriefing with the school faculty, staff, and administration. Within four weeks, a formal version of the report was distributed to the school's leadership team as well as the board and central office. The consultants worked with the group to interpret the findings and determine a course of action.

Over a three-year period, all schools participated in the inquiry experience, as did all central support offices, which were themselves studied by strategic inquiry teams. The set of reports from each of the teams formed a compelling portrait of how we were doing our work as a district. However, it wasn't the reports as much as the *process* that was important. Teachers, principals, and central office bureaucrats had the opportunity to spend a week in a school or office other than their own, trying to determine how well that school or office was doing at providing a supportive and effective learning environment. They had the chance to talk in depth about curriculum, teaching, and learning. They had the experience of crossing traditional boundaries and conventions as we all learned together. In making arrangements to be away from their positions for the week, they learned how to distribute their leadership responsibilities. And, we hoped, they all had the experience of collaborating in a process intended to improve the performance of the entire organization—a process intended to build a "corporate" culture of trust and support and to generate fresh ideas.[1]

A feature of the strategic inquiry process that needs emphasis is the experience of cross-visitation. It is easy to forget how parochial

---

[1] In the United States, school accreditation is a similar process, although it is generally restricted to high schools and happens infrequently, usually at ten-year intervals. What's different is that the visiting teams are strangers from other districts and states who are there to make summary judgments about the quality of school programs and facilities. Being on an accrediting team can be an educative experience, but the benefits do not accrue to one's home organization in the same manner as happens with strategic inquiry.

schools are, and how unusual it is for teachers and principals to ever spend any time in another school during the school day, let alone an entire week. Thus, the experience of making an extended visit to another school is itself outside the conventions of schooling and, by "making the familiar strange" (Erickson, 1987), provokes inquiry and reflection. When business office administrators spend a week in schools, and when they themselves are observed by teachers and principals, the inquiry becomes truly systemic.

In writing about school reform, Tony Wagner speaks of "change as collaborative inquiry: a constructivist methodology for reinventing schools" (1998, p. 512). He argues that it is only through processes such as the strategic inquiry initiative that substantive organizational change can happen. Our experience in Trenton certainly seems to bear out that assertion.

A Leadership Learning Community at Work: Examples

Although strategic inquiry was the most comprehensive and inclusive of our leadership development activities, several other programs deserve further explanation. An early development program was the Ventures in Leadership seminar conducted by Pat Sanaghan (a consultant who had earlier been instrumental in getting teacher contract negotiations off to a good start). Ventures was advertised across the district as a six-session after-school program open to administrators, teachers, and paraprofessionals. Sanaghan selected an intentionally diverse group from the applicant pool, then took group members through a series of role plays, simulations, and exercises designed to build leadership skills. Reaction was so positive that we repeated the series three times.

Another development experiment was the establishment of teacher networks. Because we had dissolved our curriculum office during the administrative retirement incentive program, we needed to build curriculum support capacity in another way. We put together a pool of almost $1 million from various grant sources, then advertised to our teacher workforce the opportunity to form teacher networks. Any group of teachers could form a network so long as there were participants from at least two schools and they had a purpose that built on addressing the state's core curriculum standards. Teachers would be compensated at our professional development rate ($30/hour), and one teacher in the group would act as coordinator and submit payroll forms. The group was also expected to keep minutes of their meetings and to submit reports to the central office on a quarterly basis. A number of groups quickly emerged (e.g., the librarians), and they soon established themselves as support and learning communities. (Participating in a network did not preclude being part of other professional development programs.)

One of the most successful networks was the Trenton Writing Project, associated with the National Writing Project, and organized in partnership with nearby Rider University. Teachers from across grades and subjects led summer workshops for each other, and met monthly to share lessons, student work, and their own writing and research.

The Board of Education also undertook its own long-term leadership development program. With the help of The Aspen Group, the board learned how to be a "policy governance" board, that is, a board that delegates all operational responsibility to the superintendent, then governs through policy. Rather than spend its meeting time reviewing and approving agenda items, the board adopted a very different approach. It set performance expectations for everything from student achievement to operations (e.g., building cleanliness), then used board meeting time to hear reports on how the district was responding to its direction and performing in relation to expectations.

I was personally involved in many of these activities—as a participant. I was a member of the first Ventures seminar and served on a strategic inquiry team. I attended all the policy governance training meetings. I read reports from the teacher network groups, and would sometimes visit with teachers in these groups to hear about how they were experiencing them. I wanted to make clear that I wasn't only the district leader; I was also a learner and didn't consider myself above these development programs. Being a participant had the added benefit of putting me in contact with cross sections of district employees, keeping me in touch with what they were thinking and feeling.

A Collaborative Approach to Choosing a New Math Program

During the latter part of my time in Trenton, the state Department of Education began to pull back on its mandate that schools implement state-approved programs, allowing more latitude in local curriculum control so long as state standards were addressed. Although our test scores in reading and mathematics had been showing steady improvement, we felt we could accelerate gains in math if we adopted a single program, including curriculum and textbooks. We were using at least three different approaches, but we knew that schools would be willing to consider a single district curriculum—so long as it was the one they were already using. Nevertheless, there was consensus among principals and teacher leaders that we needed a unified math program.

We were determined to make the selection decision in a collaborative and inclusive way. And we wanted to ensure that when the decision was made it would have broad support, making the selection process, in effect, the first stage in implementation. Based on a review of research on math program effectiveness and our own experience with several programs, we selected five programs for consideration. Then we announced that there would be an early evening "Math Fair" with a buffet supper, and we invited principals, teachers, parent leaders, and school board members to attend. Each of the five math programs was explained in a fifteen-minute presentation to the audience. Then the presenters moved to a display booth staffed by representatives of the publishers as well as teachers in the district who had taught the program and were proponents of it.

For an hour we visited the booths, examined the materials, and got answers to whatever questions we might have. Then the facilitators distributed ballots and asked everyone to rank their top three choices; the ballots were counted and the results announced to the group. (The choice was *Investigations in Number, Data, and Space.*) Not everyone was pleased, but no one felt the decision had been arbitrary, and everyone appreciated the transparency and openness of the process.

We moved forward to districtwide implementation, knowing that this new program would be a radical shift for many of our teachers. I attended each of the orientation meetings, advising teachers that we were well aware that it would take at least two years before they were comfortable with the new program. A year later, improved math test results indicated that our implementation strategy had borne fruit.

CAPITAL IMPROVEMENTS FOR REAL: $400+ MILLION

One of the provisions of the 1998 New Jersey Supreme Court order in the *Abbott* case was that students in urban districts should be able to go to schools that were in good enough condition and so designed that the students could be reasonably expected to learn in ways that would permit them to meet state standards. In other words, there needed to be operating heating systems, gyms, science classrooms, appropriate space for children with various special needs, and so on. The settlement in the case included $4.5 billion designated for rehabilitation of existing buildings and new school construction in urban districts and another $2 billion for suburban districts—a big carrot, not just for urban school districts, but also for construction companies, architects, labor unions, and many and varied other potentially interested parties. (And it was the largest capital program commitment for public schools of any state in the country.)

Recently I got a phone call from a reporter at the *Trenton Times* who wanted to know why the Trenton public schools had gotten proportionately more new schools and building improvements than any other city in the state. The answer may seem convoluted, but it illustrates perhaps more clearly than any other story here what being entrepreneurial means in the public sector.

Our district leadership team had a loosely stated but well-understood theory of action:

- Follow any state guidelines for Abbott school construction to the letter.
- Be first in line.
- Do *not* assume the state knows what it's doing.
- Make sure all our local constituencies are informed and on board at every step.
- Make sure we're positioned to manage (control) organizational and social networks.
- Be prepared to risk operating budget funds for planning and development costs, in hopes of high return on investment. Do *not* depend on the state for planning and development funding. Recognize that we'll need to spend money to get money.
- Keep the big picture—better school facilities—in front while celebrating every small win.

The state guidelines for project funding required an approved long-range school facilities improvement plan, which had to include demographic projections, assessments of current facilities, and estimates of future needs—all justified by their correspondence to court-mandated instructional programs.

We persuaded the Board of Education to reallocate available funds to contract with an experienced and knowledgeable local architecture and planning firm, Clark, Caton & Hintz, to develop our long-range plan. Although state regulation did not require it, we presented the plan to the City Planning Commission for approval, held a series of public meetings for plan review and comment, kept our local elected officials apprised, and submitted our plan before the deadline. Another element of our strategy was to submit our plan several weeks before the due date, ensuring that we would be first in line for review. Within months the plan was approved.

However, we understood that there was a difference between having an approved plan and having approval for specific projects. Knowing that each school construction plan was going to need approval by at least two state agencies—the Department of Education and the newly created School Construction Company (a nonprofit state authority)—we maneuvered to control the process. We suspected that the state had no established internal process for plan review or for transferring plans from one agency to another. So we hired our own expediters.

One of the expediters, Dwayne Mosley, was an employee we had recruited from the Department of Education's division of school construction. He had previously worked for a Trenton-based construction management company and already knew many of our school buildings. The other was a personal friend of mine, Dr. Ben Ashcom, recently retired from the nursing home consulting business. Ben had extensive experience with complex, government-financed construction projects, but more importantly, was a gracious and skilled glad-hander. Every time a new project was ready for submission, Dwayne and Ben would hand deliver it and then volunteer to help move it from one state office to another.

Again, in funding the positions of the expediters, the board was risking operating budget funds while recognizing that there was no assurance we would ever get the projects approved. On the other hand, the dollar cost was small, our budget was balanced, schools had the resources they had requested, and the possible return on investment seemed very much worth the risk. While most other cities were waiting for the state to help them get their long-range plans done, we figured that help would be a long time coming.

The third and most important investment by the board was to approve leases or options for every abandoned but serviceable Catholic school building in the city. That meant we had readily available swing space, so we could rapidly relocate entire schools when a project required it. The board and I knew that even though we might recover the lease costs from the state in the long run, we had to take the risk ahead of time so that project approval wouldn't be delayed because we had nowhere for kids to go while their schools were being rehabilitated or replaced.

The next steps were more obvious. First, we formed a facilities advisory board with monthly meetings open to anyone; at these meetings, we provided continuing updates on program and project status and listened to concerns from the community. Given the size of the projects and the business and employment opportunities the projects would generate, it wasn't difficult to organize community participation. For example, among the concerned citizens who regularly attended were members of the local clergy who cared deeply about minority participation in the projects, whether in the skilled trades, small businesses, or project management.

The advisory board's actions were ongoing and carefully targeted:

- Keep our local elected officials in the loop, and have them lobby and advocate as might be required.
- Advocate for awarding architecture and construction contracts to firms that we knew or suspected had enough political clout that they could work with us to secure project approval.
- Conduct monthly coordination and implementation meetings at the superintendent's office with all the players in the room at the same time—state agencies, construction management companies, architects and planners, and key internal staff—with the implicit understanding that the state was under heavy pressure to get projects underway as quickly as possible.
- Keep the pressure on the School Construction Corporation to approve and fund our projects, reminding them that their success would ultimately be measured by getting schools built.
- Jump every time the governor's office called and wanted a picture of the governor cutting a ribbon.

The results were dramatic—more than $400 million invested in new schools, additions, and improvements.

ACCEPTING OUR CHANGING RELATIONSHIP WITH THE STATE

In an essay on leadership and school improvement, Richard Elmore argues that standards-based reform "undermines a basic premise of local governance of education. Schools are the primary unit of accountability in virtually all state accountability systems, not school districts" (2000, p. 9). He goes on to explain the states have dramatically expanded their "capacity to collect, analyze and report data on individual schools" and to apply "remedies and sanctions" to low-performing schools (p. 9). As this relationship between state departments of education and schools evolves (particularly in urban districts), Elmore contends, the purposes of local boards of education and central administrative offices will come increasingly into question unless their contributions to school performance are clear. These arguments certainly applied in some ways to our experience in Trenton, where the board increasingly felt its role preempted by the Department of Education. And my own role as superintendent was at many times that of intermediary between the department and the schools. Yet our success as a district in many respects related to our ability to manage and outmaneuver the state, a possibility that Elmore apparently had not considered.

9

High School Reform

Although the state's Abbott urban school reform agenda focused on preschool and early elementary grades, and the department of education acknowledged that it had no comprehensive strategy for improving high schools, the most dramatic changes in Trenton during my superintendency occurred at the high school level. There were two significant components: redesigning the city's large comprehensive and iconic high school and opening a "dropout recovery" program, which was successful well beyond our expectations.

REORGANIZING AND REFORMING A LARGE COMPREHENSIVE HIGH SCHOOL

One of the primary reasons I was hired as superintendent in Trenton was because I had successfully transformed a large urban high school into small learning communities (SLCs), and in the process improved its climate, graduation rate, and standardized test scores, and increased its enrollment. Shortly after I was appointed in Trenton, the mayor made it clear to me that there were "too many young people hanging on the corners," and he wanted them back in school and on track to productive lives.

With that goal in mind, I spent a good deal of time at Trenton Central High School during my early months as superintendent. Trenton Central High had a proud tradition dating back to the late nineteenth century. But as local industry collapsed and the middle class moved to the suburbs, the school followed a familiar path of decline—white students disappeared, minority students struggled and resisted, the faculty yearned for the good old days, and the school descended into the abyss. Although only 30 percent of entering ninth graders made it to graduation, a substantial majority of the faculty believed that they were doing their jobs. In their view, the problem was that the students weren't taking advantage of their opportunities.

Before my arrival, the school had been involved in a "reform" planning project for three years that called for subdividing the building into smaller units, but none of the plans had been implemented. My observations and analysis convinced me that the faculty and administration were willing to let the situation drag on forever. In February, I had a one-on-one conference with the principal. He acknowledged that he was not the right person to lead the school through reform. He had been asked to become principal eight years earlier because of his reputation as a good disciplinarian and no-nonsense leader at one of the district middle schools. He suggested that I reassign him to a parallel position in the central office, where he could work until his retirement in two years. Conveniently, we had a vacancy in the director of student services position, and he agreed to take it. A week later, he went out on long-term sick leave, making me the *de facto* high school principal while we searched for a replacement.

In every principalship position I had held before going to Trenton, I had headed schools that were organized in SLCs or that I had helped reorganize into SLCs. My experience was that SLCs created close, personal relationships between teachers and students, and encouraged teachers to collaborate in creating supportive learning communities. I didn't think SLCs were necessarily the solution for all schools, but I was reasonably confident that they would improve the conditions at Trenton Central High School.

In meetings with the school's administrative team, faculty representatives, student government, and school management team, I made it clear that the school would be reorganized into SLCs by September, in keeping with the reform plan the school had been developing. There was a good deal of grumbling, but I moved forward with the reorganization plans. A week before spring vacation, student leaders advised me that they were planning a walkout on the Friday before the holiday to protest the reorganization. As the students shared their concerns, it became clear that a number of teachers were instigating the walkout and feeding them misinformation about the proposed redesign of the school.

By happenstance, on the morning of the planned walkout I was at the school early for a meeting concerning a possible culinary program. When the meeting concluded about 8:15, I walked toward the main office and was amazed that the building was so quiet. No one was in the halls. I walked to the main entrance and opened the door. There on the front lawn were 1,500 students and many adults, some carrying protest signs. Across the street were several police cars, the officers surveying the scene, dogs on leashes. I had two thoughts: "Today may be my last day in Trenton," and "If I don't take charge of this situation, there is a real possibility of disaster." So I walked to the front of the patio and began talking to the students. They were shouting their objections, and I was trying to respond. Most of the crowd couldn't hear anything other than the sounds of protest. Then from somewhere a bullhorn appeared. The student leaders and I took turns as we worked our way through their issues. At one point part of the group turned to march to city hall, and much to my relief turned back when the police blocked their way. None of the faculty or staff was out on the lawn, although some watched from windows on the upper floors.

The protest had gone on for over an hour when I urged the group to move into the school auditorium so we could all hear each other. They agreed, and in we went. A microphone was set up and the dialogue continued. The key issue seemed to be that the eleventh graders didn't want to be split up into separate communities for their senior year. I agreed that we could keep them together and not implement the entire reorganization until the following year. The students were also reassured to know that each SLC would provide a college prep curriculum. Sometime after 11:00, we agreed that we were tired and had gone as far as we could. I promised to provide the student government a written statement of our agreements on reorganization on the Monday following the holiday. The students went off to the cafeteria, and I took a deep breath. The next day the local newspapers printed headline stories praising the students for their mature behavior.

When school reopened on the Monday following spring break, I called an emergency faculty meeting. I was furious with the faculty for putting the kids at risk. They had all hidden in the building and sent the students out to do the protesting—with the police waiting to bang heads. I told them that they had forfeited their authority. The kids were the ones who were acting responsibly. It didn't matter whether the faculty agreed with the proposed reorganization; what mattered was their willingness to engage the issues. The faculty had been willing to accept a 70 percent dropout rate and unwilling to accept responsibility for making the school work for all its students. Their resistance was broken, and we moved forward with the reorganization.

Teachers were invited to develop proposals for SLCs and to recruit colleagues. In early May we had a selection fair. The students decided which communities they wanted to be part of, and only those that attracted enough students to justify support were allowed to move forward. In a sense, the kids had taken control of the reorganization.

Three years later the graduation rate had doubled, test scores were up, and the school climate had changed from prison to learning community. Teachers who had opposed the reorganization were now its advocates.

In retrospect, I feel good about what we accomplished, but I do take pause at how close we came to disaster. And how did I explain to myself what had happened? I recognize that Ron Heifetz (1994) is right: It's very difficult for adults or kids to give up the known for the unknown. Or, to put it in the language of chaos and complexity theory: "Where the dominant attractor pattern is sustaining an undesirable state, the challenge will be to open the door to instability, or even to *create* the instability that will help a new pattern of behavior emerge" (Morgan, 1997, p. 269).

DAYLIGHT/TWILIGHT: PUTTING ABBOTT TO WORK

As I mentioned earlier, Trenton's mayor, Doug Palmer, had let me know that his first priority was to get young people off the street corners and back into school or gainful employment. As principal at University City High School in Philadelphia, I had been involved with an after-school dropout recovery program that allowed dropouts to re-enroll and attend classes from 4:00 to 8:00 p.m. Monday through Friday evenings. The teacher leader running the program, Bill Tracy, had had reasonable success in getting some rather sketchy characters to return to school, make up the classes they had failed, and earn enough credits to graduate. I admired Bill's concern for these young people and his ability to set high expectations for them with a sense of humor.

The solution to the Trenton mayor's challenge seemed to me to be to create a school whose only students were adults and young people—the ones who had left school before meeting graduation requirements, whether because of boredom, being overaged for their grade, needing to support themselves or family, teen pregnancy and parenthood, caring for other family members, or criminal activity.

Something from Nothing

The *Abbott* court decision mandated creation of alternative programs for students not succeeding in regular programs, so we had state policy cover. I persuaded the school board to lease an abandoned parochial school as the site for this new alternative school and to hire Bill Tracy as principal. But in the manner of "creative insubordination" (Morris, Crowson, Porter-Gehrie, & Hurwitz, 1984), we did not ask the state Department of Education for permission to start a new school. Instead, we made it an annex of the district's comprehensive high school and simply reallocated resources (i.e., teachers and books) from the main building, so we did not require new funding beyond the lease cost.

When Bill and I began to lay out the design for the new program—Daylight/Twilight—we didn't try to solve the problem by creating a new dropout prevention program or "fixing" the existing high school. Instead, we made several key assumptions:

- If the dropout rate had been almost 70 percent for the last decade, then there were a lot of folks in town who had never finished high school.
- Being out on the street for a year or two concentrates the attention. Young people begin to understand how hard it is to get a job without a diploma.
- The new school (or annex, for the time being) had to accommodate the lifestyles of prospective students. It could not replicate the organization that had failed these individuals and in which they had failed. And it had to allow for work or child care schedules.
- The program had to demonstrate respect for every student and quickly earn their trust—or they'd be gone.
- Finally, it had to be safe.

Without getting into too much detail about the features of Daylight/Twilight, I will list just a few that probably contributed to its quick success:

- Prospective students had to be at least seventeen years old and out of school for at least six months (so as not to draw enrollment from the traditional high school).
- Students could choose one of three "shifts" to attend: 7:30–11:30 a.m., 12:00–4:00 p.m., or 5:00–9:00 p.m.
- During any four-hour shift there were three class meeting periods, each one hour and fifteen minutes long.
- There were four ten-week quarters and a summer session. Students could enroll at the beginning of any quarter.

- More than three absences in a quarter or a major disciplinary infraction was cause for immediate dismissal, but those excluded could re-enroll at the beginning of the next quarter.
- Transcripts from all previous high school enrollments were reviewed to determine what courses and credits students needed to earn to meet graduation requirements. In addition, work histories were reviewed to determine whether "life experience" credit could be awarded. The goal was to help students meet all their requirements as quickly as possible.
- There was no lunch period and no physical education classes. There were no electives except those that could be taken online.
- Any course could be taken and completed online. We contracted with Advanced Academics, an accredited virtual high school based in Oklahoma, to provide their catalog of courses, which students could take in the computer lab, at the public library, or at home (at $300 per course per student, less than our cost).
- Each student took only the courses needed to complete graduation requirements.
- The location, an old parochial elementary school, was several miles from Trenton Central High, so there were no encounters with students or faculty from the "old" school.

By the second year, Daylight/Twilight enrollment was over 1,500 students per quarter, and we began to open satellites in other facilities around the city. More than a third of the students were adults, ranging in age up to seventy years old. The number of graduates quickly climbed to almost five hundred annually, more than from the comprehensive high school—helping us triple the number of city residents receiving high school diplomas each year. (At one Daylight/Twilight graduation a grandmother, her daughter, and her three granddaughters all received diplomas. They were featured in a front-page story in the *Trenton Times*.)

In a recent book on disruptive innovation in education, Christensen, Horn, and Johnson (2008) provide a perspective on change in schools, describing how their research on innovation in the corporate sectors suggests possibilities for the education sector. Although much of the book deals with the power of new technologies to provide individualized learning options, it also addresses the question why innovation has been so difficult in education and sets out principles for successful innovation. These principles have helped me understand how and why we were able to create Daylight/Twilight so quickly, why it was so successful, and why it has encountered barriers a decade after its inception.

Christensen et al. are emphatic that "a disruptive innovation is *not* a breakthrough improvement" (2008, p. 47). Rather, it "brings to market a good or service that is actually not as good as what companies historically had been selling. Because it is not as good, the existing customers . . . cannot use it. But by making the product affordable and simple to use, the disruptive innovation benefits people who had been unable to consume the [traditional] product—people we call 'nonconsumers.'"

By targeting those who had already dropped out, Daylight/Twilight was clearly focusing on nonconsumers and not competing with the regular high school. The students the program was designed to serve were the ones no one wanted; they had been expelled from the regular school or left of their own accord. They were perceived to be difficult, resistant, and undeserving.

By eliminating many of the conventional features of high schools— elective courses, physical education classes, the library, and lunch programs—we were providing a service that was "not as good" as the regular program. But we were also sharply reducing costs by using leased or donated space, part-time faculty, and online courses, and by limiting or eliminating remedial and social service programs, security and discipline staffing, cafeteria staff, and so forth. A concurrent benefit of the program was that we were rapidly increasing enrollment in the district, compensating for years of declining enrollment, and ensuring that our state subsidy payments would increase (because the state didn't understand what a low-cost school might look like).

How had we done this so easily? According to Christensen et al., the culture and conventions of most organizations make disruptive innovation (e.g., products such as the Toyota Prius) impossible unless organizations create "heavyweight teams" that can "transcend the boundaries of their functional organizations and interact in different ways" (2008, p. 204). These teams must work in separate locations outside the primary organization, bring "functional expertise" with them, and have a manager with "significant clout" to lead the team.

The "heavyweight team" that created Daylight/Twilight was almost invisible. We had an outsider as principal, the director of our security division as recruiter, and the superintendent as the manager/ sponsor and functional expert (because I knew a lot about alternative high school programs). The site was a leased Catholic elementary school that had been abandoned because of declining enrollments—a minimalist facility. In most apparent respects, the new program wasn't a threat to any of the existing programs.

Christensen et al. maintain that when managers are trying to develop a "disruptive business model innovation," they need to create an "autonomous business unit" because existing units within the company "cannot prioritize [an innovation] relative to other investments they have the option of making" (2008, p. 205). In other words, if the same resources were made available to the regular high school program, they would quickly be absorbed in reduced class size, remedial programs, staff development, and so forth—none of which would disrupt anything. Within a year of its start-up, Daylight/Twilight had been so successful that the Board of Education and the state Department of Education had no choice but to accept it as a stand-alone school rather than an annex, and we were able to spin it off as an autonomous business unit.

Demonstrating Success

With accountability and assessment such prominent features of current education policy, an important question for Daylight/Twilight was how it could demonstrate that it was meeting state and local standards. The first criterion is obvious—its students had to earn the required number of course credits (four credits in English, three in math, etc.). Then they had to pass New Jersey's high-stakes high school exit exam in reading and mathematics. But in recognition that some sort of adaptation might be necessary for some students, New Jersey has also created the special review assessment (SRA), a test that requires students who have been unsuccessful on the standard exam to complete a series of individualized tasks over a period of several weeks. The SRA is a secure test, and student responses are reviewed by two teachers independently, then forwarded to the county superintendent for certification. We were careful to adhere to these procedures, and we were able to use the SRA exam process for a majority of our prospective graduates.

Anticipating that there might be complaints about Daylight/Twilight's performance because it was so successful and so unconventional—and because so many of its students were meeting the exit exam requirement through the SRA—we were careful to do follow-up surveys of graduates. We determined that at least 90 percent were working, in college, or both. Considering that this was a client population that had been discarded, this rate seemed to us to point to a remarkable success story and to constitute evidence that we were doing what the state Supreme Court had intended in its Abbott order. And it didn't hurt that Principal Bill Tracy was soon being asked to go to conferences and hearings in Washington, D.C., to explain how we had been able to address the dropout issue.

In the words of David Hargreaves, we were successful because we were able to "rethink fundamental assumptions about what works or is possible," to introduce new or better quality goods, and to improve "educational productivity, efficiency, and quality" (2003a, p. 2). In the terminology of Hargreaves, we had implemented a high-leverage strategy, which produced "a large outcome in terms of quality and/or quantity for a minimal investment" (p. 5).

THE BIG QUESTIONS

With Abbott-mandated and local reforms going on in so many directions and at so many levels, not just in high schools, it would have been easy to get so caught up in reforming that we forgot to pay attention to the *big* questions: Was all this reform making any difference for our students? How did we know? What was the evidence? That is the subject of the next chapter.

🔟

To What End?

One of the reasons I was encouraged to write this book is that over the course of my career I have developed a reputation as a reformer and risk-taker who has been consistently able to increase opportunities and improve performance for students in troubled schools and districts. In telling the story of my experience in Trenton, I have tried to share how I and my colleagues worked to make a difference for Trenton's children and for the community. In many ways we had remarkable success. But there is also a postscript to the story, and it directly addresses the question of sustainability of urban school reform.

FRAMING CHANGE AS DRIVEN BY MORAL PURPOSE

Fullan (1993, 1999) contends that our increasing understanding of chaos and complexity theory suggests that "planned" educational change is in fact not predictable—that detailed planning is futile. In his view, change driven by moral purpose has a much higher probability of success than change driven by standards and mandates.

As superintendent, I developed two complementary strategies to build support for change. One was to emphasize that our primary mission was ensuring that as many students as possible who entered ninth grade completed high school and went on to college, work, or military service (or combinations of the three). I regularly reminded everyone that what parents and the community wanted—more than higher test scores—was for their children to become responsible, self-supporting adults. That is why we redesigned the high school into career-oriented small learning communities, each with college, community organization, and corporate partners, and why we initiated dropout recovery and adult high school programs.

My mantra was that we had no excuses. The district had every element necessary to ensure that the kids were successful—adequate funding, strong political support, agreements with employees that supported reform, a board committed to the best interests of children, capable leadership, a positive organizational climate, and partnerships with a wide array of local educational, corporate, business, and social service organizations.

The other strategy was to focus on "noxiants" (see Morgan, 1997), the long-standing problems that need to be reduced or eliminated to improve performance and opportunities for students. The list included an extraordinary dropout rate, a high incidence of special education referrals, an undue use of suspension as a disciplinary strategy, high rates of retention in grade, high course and subject failure rates, and high failure rates on the high school proficiency test. All of these indicators are ones over which schools have control, all are demonstrated by research to relate to negative student outcomes, and all are areas where we quickly showed improvement (e.g., doubling the number of high school graduates in one year, and reducing suspensions by over 50 percent in two years).

Because of the district's commitment to leadership development, its participation in a number of state and national development programs, and its association with cutting-edge mid-career doctoral programs, Trenton had the additional benefits of attracting outstanding young minority administrators and of identifying, developing, and promoting equally strong internal minority candidates. (Over 30 percent of the school and central office administrative staff were thirty-five or younger, and 95 percent of that group were African American or Hispanic.)

We made a concerted effort to recruit, develop, promote, and support administrators and teacher leaders who had a deep sense of commitment to increasing opportunities for the children of the city. A substantial majority of the administrative appointments to principal, vice principal, and central office positions were African Americans or Latinos, and a majority of them came from outside the district—many from sectors other than K–12 school systems. They were attracted to Trenton because we were purpose-driven and were willing to invest in their continuing development. Interestingly, much of the credit for their selection belonged to school management teams who consistently recommended the strongest of the available candidates, not simply the insider they already knew.

ON THE RIGHT PATH

As Trenton's approach to leadership development evolved, it became increasingly integrated into the district's organizational and performance improvement work, extending from a deepening understanding of what was happening in classrooms through to a coordinated district and state collaboration in helping the school board take a more active role in leading for improved student achievement. In designing its leadership development programs, the district chose a fluid and adaptive approach that was both job-embedded and program-specific, and that addressed leadership across the employee and client spectrum.

Trenton might be considered an example of next-generation approaches to leadership development because the district made relatively limited use of area colleges and universities. The primary relationships were with independent consultants and nonprofit organizations with experience in the corporate, social service, and educational sectors. The reasons included strong client orientation, breadth and depth of experience, and willingness to customize services.[1]

Without suggesting a causal relationship, in many respects the improvements in performance in Trenton during my time there were dramatic. For example, the number of high school graduates tripled (from fewer than three hundred in 1998 to almost nine hundred in 2006), the high school attrition rate was reduced by 300 percent (from 60 percent to 18 percent), and student performance on elementary-grade state reading tests improved from 23 percent to 69 percent of general education students meeting state standards. We had also made $400 million in capital improvements. A reasonable assumption would be that the school board was pleased, if not ecstatic. We were on the path to sustainable improvement.

SUSTAINABILITY, OR REFLECTING ON FAILURE

In *Sustainable Leadership,* Andy Hargreaves and Dean Fink define leadership that fosters sustainability in the following manner: "Sustainable educational leadership and improvement preserves and develops deep learning for all that spreads and lasts, in ways that do no

---

[1] Although Trenton may be unusual in the sense that it had significant financial support through its Wallace Foundation and federal leadership program grants, most urban districts have sufficient funding through No Child Left Behind/Elementary and Secondary Education Act Titles I and II to duplicate Trenton's programs if they choose to do so.

harm and indeed create positive benefit for others around us, now and in the future" (2006, p. 17).

As a leader, whether principal or superintendent, one would like to think that the improvements one has fostered will be sustained. In the account of my tenure in Trenton I have tried to illustrate how I went about developing deep learning, and I have pointed to improvements in organizational performance that are evidence of positive benefit. Yet in the short time since I left Trenton, much of what I accomplished there has already been dismantled, and the district has regressed to the point where it is again a candidate for state intervention. On my departure, I told my successor that I would be at his disposal should he want my help, but otherwise I would stay away and give him the chance to make his own way. (He has never called.) Even though I have tried to maintain a careful distance and have been occupied with a new job, some former colleagues stay in touch, two have been my graduate students, and I have been witness in a dismissal trial and defendant in another trial, so the district remains in my life.

As superintendent in Trenton, I had worked with the school board to develop a coherent approach to district governance. With support from the Wallace Foundation and training by consultants from The Aspen Group, we wrote policies that would "hold staff accountable for all internal actions and release staff to concentrate their time and efforts on student achievement" (Dawson & Quinn, 2004, p. 29). We provided support for board members as they attended a variety of regional, national, and even international conferences and programs. By every indication, the board had embraced opportunities for deep learning.

From the outset of my superintendency in Trenton, I had also made sure to keep the mayor informed of my plans and challenges, and he and I developed a comfortable working relationship. He was in his third term, a charismatic and very popular leader who was working hard to rebuild a distressed city. He regularly praised the district's accomplishments, and he joined with me in pressing the state and federal governments for additional support. The city and the district collaborated on everything from after-school and summer recreation programs to juvenile violence prevention and snow removal.

In anticipation of my retirement, I had built a strong administrative team with at least three prospective candidates for superintendent among them. When I left, the district was on a positive course—improving student test scores, increasing high school graduation rates, improved school climate, increasing enrollments, a balanced budget, and employee contracts in place. A highly respected national search firm had been retained to help the board identify my successor.

Over the course of eight years, I had worked with four board presidents, and with each change of board leadership tensions between me and the board had increased to some degree as the new presidents injected their personal agendas into their roles. As an example, the last of the four had political ambitions, including running for mayor, and was using his position for public posturing rather than focusing on the interests of the students. Nevertheless, my relationships with the board presidents had not prevented us from moving a reform agenda forward and dealing with state and federal mandates. Generally, all seemed reasonably well.

Just before my departure, however, the board selected an external candidate for superintendent whose credentials didn't match those of any of the internal candidates, and then quickly moved to demote the senior administrators I had groomed for the position. Over the next year, the board carried out a series of vendettas, including demotions and dismissals, creating the impression that any of the "outsiders" I'd recruited were tainted by their association with me. The new superintendent rapidly came to be perceived as the board's pawn. And successful programs (e.g., small learning communities at the high school) were dismantled with no concern that they had clearly been successful.

From afar, I blamed a faction of the board that I viewed as embittered. And I blamed the mayor, because the board members are appointed by the mayor. I had done my best for eight years, there was substantial evidence of dramatic improvement, and if the board wanted to revert to their petty ways and let the district sink, then that was the mayor's fault, not mine. "Once you're gone, you're gone," I told myself.

I might look back to Hargreaves and Fink for some degree of solace: "Sustainable educational leadership and improvement preserves and develops deep learning for all that spreads and lasts" (2006, p. 17). Maybe the principals and teachers who were involved in the array of learning opportunities provided during my term as superintendent continue to make use of that knowledge in their day-to-day practice. But in objective terms, many of the improvements made during my years of service have not been sustained.

Had I not been writing this book, I probably could have avoided trying to make sense of what has happened. But I teach that we learn from our failures, so what have I learned while reflecting on my time in Trenton?

I have already mentioned that the district had a leadership development grant from the Wallace Foundation and that a requirement of the grant was participation in a leadership seminar at the Kennedy

School of Government at Harvard, conducted by Ron Heifetz, psychiatrist and author of *Leadership on the Line* (2002, coauthored with Marty Linsky) and *Leadership Without Easy Answers* (1994). What I wrote about that experience still rings true today:

> The answer [to dilemmas in our districts] was within us. We had to act on what we were learning. For me this has meant dealing with people and situations I'd rather avoid; acknowledging my discomfort with conflict; recognizing my tendency to intellectualize and analyze rather than just do it; admitting that for all my espoused comfort with chaos and complexity, I still have a need to control (better to lead than to follow); and sensing when I am reverting to my comfort zone. (Lytle, 2004, p. 25)

As I think about what has happened in Trenton since my departure, I don't think I worked hard enough at managing the board or the mayor. I believed that if I was doing a good job, and district performance was improving, then that was sufficient. But I didn't work at developing personal relationships with each of the board members, I didn't recruit new board members for the mayor to consider as possible appointments, and I didn't spend enough time schmoozing a gregarious mayor. I didn't go to the school board meeting in Atlantic City each year and socialize with board members. I didn't send them birthday cards or have a meal with each of them at regular intervals.

I was cordial and respectful, but in some ways I was probably perceived as aloof. I was white in a black city. I was an Ivy Leaguer in a working-class and welfare-dependent town. Most weekends I spent in Philadelphia, not Trenton. I didn't attend a local church. I was good at public events, connected to community organizations, and passionate about making things better for kids, but I didn't observe the local social conventions. I stayed within my comfort zone.

If I had worked harder at my relationships with the board and the mayor, would more of what I had helped put in place still *be* in place? Who can say? Presidents, governors, mayors, and CEOs wrestle with similar questions as they reflect on their own terms in office.

But I still take great satisfaction in what I accomplished in Trenton—especially the three thousand high school students and dropouts who earned diplomas and who otherwise would not have been graduates. Yes, test scores went up, school climate improved, discipline problems declined—but what mattered most, by far, was improving students' prospects and seeing the families of the graduates celebrating their success.

AN INTERPRETATION

In his discussion of organizations as "psychic prisons" Morgan (1997) cites the work of Eric Trist, who studied coal miners in Britain. Trist discovered that "the habit of working in 'bad systems' had the compensation of allowing many workers to leave some of their own sense of 'badness' in the system" (pp. 246–247). Although "they hated their work, they could not change it. The system had a strange way of tying them in." Morgan continues, "In a similar way, people may build a dependency on some aspect of culture or social life that leads them to resist innovations that would undermine this dependency, even though in terms of 'logical' criteria change seems the right thing for all concerned."

Morgan and Trist's insights have helped me understand some of what has transpired since I left Trenton, as the school system has been caught up in crises and criticism.

I remember once having a conversation with Mayor Palmer, just the two of us sitting in his office, when he told me that his biggest challenge was to get the people of Trenton to believe that things could be better. My interpretation of the mayor's comment is that the city had been in decline for so long that its people had developed what Martin Seligman (1975) calls "learned helplessness." A majority of the school board members couldn't accept the fact that we had become successful, that we were doing many things well. They could not leave the "badness." In trying to comprehend why the school board would begin to dismantle obviously successful reforms, this is the best explanation I have been able to generate.

Perhaps that explains why one of my current interests is leadership transitions, both for superintendents and principals (see Lytle, 2009). In my experience, leadership transitions are fragile times in organizations, whether schools or districts, and are often badly managed, both by those doing the hiring and by the candidates. Yet smooth and well-planned transitions have a great deal to do with an organization's continuing improvement and long-term success.

III

LEADERSHIP FOR LEARNING

Considering the
Teaching of Leadership

One of the benefits of writing a book based on one's career is that it creates an opportunity to pull together pieces and parts, to make connections among experiences, to reflect back on a career, and to see whether coherent patterns and themes emerge. Although what I have written is certainly autobiographical, and represented from my recollections and perspectives, I've tried to keep in mind the challenges and dilemmas facing educational leaders today and for the foreseeable future.

BEING A PROFESSOR: TEACHING LEADERSHIP

In thinking about the book I have continually asked myself: Is what I'm writing consistent with what and how I teach? In any administrative position I've held, I have always considered myself a teacher first. And I have been teaching graduate students interested in leadership and educational reform since my enforced "sabbatical" more than twenty years ago. I "retired" when I left Philadelphia and when I left Trenton, which made me a pensioner in two states. I'm a Social Security recipient, and here I am with another full-time job—teaching school.

For more than two decades, I have been an adjunct faculty member or (now) full-time practice professor in the University of Pennsylvania's Graduate School of Education. I have taught undergraduates and masters and doctoral students and chaired dissertations. During most of that time I was also a principal or superintendent, and I cannot state strongly enough how important it has been to me to do this teaching. Course planning, keeping up with the literature, reading papers, counseling, and mentoring students have all enhanced my effectiveness as an administrator because teaching outside the organization where I was the leader helped me maintain perspective. Whether my students are from China or Mississippi, exclusive private schools or the inner city, the Army or the corporate sector, they make me see the world in different ways.

That capacity ties back to Morgan's argument that:

> Skilled leaders and managers develop the knack of reading situations with various scenarios in mind and of forging actions that seem appropriate to the understandings thus obtained. They have the capacity to remain open and flexible, suspending immediate judgment whenever possible, until a more comprehensive view of the situation emerges [what Heifetz calls "ripening"]. . . . [A] wide and varied reading can create a wide and varied range of action possibilities. Less effective managers and problem solvers, however, seem to interpret everything from a fixed standpoint . . . and hit blocks they can't get around. (1997, pp. 3–4)

The stories I have told about my evolution as a leader and my work in many different settings have been meant to illustrate this argument.

Teaching a Course in Educational Leadership

Although I have spent much of my career teaching and mentoring leaders and prospective leaders, it has only been in the last three years that I have actually conducted a whole course on educational leadership. Planning and designing it have made me confront a question my students regularly ask me: Can leadership be taught? Of course I think the answer is yes, but I'm also aware of how much advantage students have who have been leaders in high school and college, and in out-of-school activities and jobs.

In developing the course, I have drawn on my work with the Wallace Foundation as well as a lifetime of research, teaching, and experience. I have tried to provide a framework or logic to help the students reflect on their evolution as leaders, think about their aspirations, and consider the prospective learning that will get them to where they want to be.

We begin with getting in touch. Each student is asked to consider:

1. His or her experience as a leader (and follower) from early childhood forward
2. Articulating a teaching point of view: Who am I? Who are you? Where are we going? How will I help us get there? (See Tichy, 2002.)

3. Considering persona: The centrality of trust, purpose, emotional intelligence, humility, and service

We then consider the unique challenges of educational leadership:

4. Understanding instructional leadership
5. Learning the context; understanding where you are
6. Establishing the conditions for leading, working, and learning
7. Distributing leadership

Finally we move to expanding horizons and repertoire:

8. Imagining different ways to lead (and to teach others to lead)
9. Leading change (and understanding resistance, danger, technical versus adaptive solutions, etc.)
10. Willingness to risk; entrepreneurship
11. Managing leadership transitions: Yours and those of others

To help my students make this journey, I use a variety of teaching methods, all intended to provoke inquiry, reflection, and self-examination, including:

- Reading in the literatures of organizational theory, leadership, and schools as organizations, as well as contrasting literatures—including business, the military, churches, nonprofits, the arts, and sports
- Role plays and simulations
- Cases, both written and on DVD
- Blackboard and other e-learning technologies
- The personal experiences of group members
- Group journals chronicling the experience in the course and the insights the course provokes
- Stories from my own experience

Other Graduate Courses

In addition to educational leadership, I teach other graduate courses as well, and my approach to them (naturally) also incorporates parts of my thinking about leadership and change.

Organizational Theory

Using Gareth Morgan's (1997) book *Images of Organization* as the central text, we try to increase our capacity to "see" schools and school systems. The premise of the course is that one's ability to act in or on organizations is facilitated by one's capacity to "read" them from different perspectives. Because most of us have spent most of our lives going to and working in schools, the challenge of seeing schools from new perspectives is held to be particularly difficult.

School Finance

The central questions of this course relate to tying resources to instructional programs and organizational priorities. The premise is that barriers to educational reform often build from the claim that "there is no money," or, alternatively, that "there isn't time." The challenge is to be clear about what and where the resources are (money, people, time, space) and then figure out how they might be reallocated.

Urban School Reform

This course is limited to Teach for America corps members just finishing their first year of teaching. Predictably, the corps members tend to be idealistic and impatient; their inclination is to change policy to improve practice. The course takes a different stance, arguing that true reform needs to begin in one's classroom and move out from there. We use each teacher's classroom and school as data sources, and consider what reform might look like in these settings. In a sense, this course incorporates the premises of the other two—that reform is contingent on learning to see and on identifying and reallocating resources. Both are significant leadership challenges, whether from one's classroom or as principal or superintendent.

The Mid-Career Doctoral Program

One of my great satisfactions over the past eight years has been to be part of a group of faculty members and practitioners at Penn's Graduate School of Education who have conceptualized and put in place a doctoral program for experienced educational leaders who choose at a mid-point in their careers to return to graduate school to earn a doctorate in educational leadership. The program operates in an executive education format with classes one weekend a month and two weeks in the summer. Students are admitted in cohorts of about twenty-five and take three years to complete their degrees. Since its inception, the program has attracted a wonderfully diverse group of applicants, both in terms of race, ethnicity, gender, religion, and place of residence, and in terms of their current jobs. A typical cohort includes a balance of students from public, private, parochial, and charter schools, as well as nonprofit organizations and even teacher union leadership. They are principals, headmasters, superintendents, charter school directors, and state department of education administrators from across the country.

By their own admission, they are at a point in their careers where they acknowledge that they have much to learn if they are going to be able to provide the kinds of leadership that will make them effective in the increasingly complex conditions they face. What makes teaching this group so exciting is the degree to which they teach each other. As an example, when I teach school finance to this group, the public school administrators assume that they operate in challenging conditions—that is, until they learn about the private school challenges like tuition pricing, yield management, development offices, and capital campaigns. In teaching this group, I often feel that my real role is facilitating the possible synergies that the group's diversity provides.

Re-Engaged with Philadelphia

In my current role as practice professor, I have a somewhat unusual responsibility. My employer, the Graduate School of Education at the University of Pennsylvania, is an education management organization (EMO) on contract to the School District of Philadelphia to provide management oversight services to two inner-city elementary schools not far from the University campus. Because the faculty members who were initially responsible for the EMO duties have all left the University to take other positions, I have backed into the job of EMO coordinator (I had sworn never to take responsibility for any organization when I retired from Trenton—so much for promises.)

In my role, I manage an array of consulting and support services for the two schools, work with the school principals in determining which programs and supports will best address their schools needs, and interact with the district's central office around their expectations for the two schools.

The schools are typically under-resourced urban schools with the added burden of a teachers' contract that eliminates after-school faculty meetings. Each month there is an early dismissal for a two-hour professional development session; in addition, there are two professional development days during the school year. One of the questions the principals and I are wrestling with is finding time to talk with teachers about teaching, curriculum, and learning issues. (In my work in Trenton, and in each school I have headed, I made it a priority to ensure weekly dedicated time for teachers to talk; bringing about change without time to talk simply isn't possible.)

Mike Schmoker makes the argument persuasively: "There is broad, even remarkable, concurrence among members of the research community on the effects of carefully structured learning teams on the improvement of instruction" (2004, p. 430). Then, quoting Judith Warren Little, he adds, "'school improvement is most surely and thoroughly achieved when teachers engage in frequent, continuous, and increasingly complex talk about teaching practice . . . adequate to the complexities of teaching, capable of distinguishing one practice and its virtue from another.'" If research suggests that a productive strategy would be to do everything to help principals learn how to provide time for, plan, and facilitate teacher meetings, and to develop teacher leaders who can also play this role, then one would assume that this would be the priority for the school district in its supervision and evaluation of principals. Instead, the principals we work with feel torn in a hundred directions as the central office bombards them with directives, requests for reports, compliance and monitoring reviews, operational responsibilities, and performance assessments with more than thirty indicators that are supposed to improve by June.

HOW CURRENT POLICY CONSTRAINS THE "MEANING-MAKING" PROCESS

The stories of my experiences have been intended to illustrate the complexity and the possibilities of school and district leadership, and to address questions I continually ask myself:

- Why did I choose to do this work?
- How did I learn to do what I have done?
- How can leaders be developed, supported, coached, and evaluated in ways that help them continue to grow, become increasingly effective, and be able to adapt to changing conditions?

In telling the story of my evolution as a school leader, one of my goals has been to establish that my knowledge, experience, and success qualify me to critique the educational leadership field. So, let the critique begin.

As I cross between the worlds of the ivory tower and inner-city schools, I can't avoid the question of how schools can best serve children.

My concern is that our current preoccupation with test scores and performance targets assumes essentially cybernetic feedback models that generate predictable school improvement and corrective action plans. But, as Morgan explains, in cybernetic systems "the learning abilities thus defined are limited in that the system can only maintain the course of action determined by the operating norms or standards guiding it" (1997, p. 86). So when performance in middle-grade reading test scores declines, the automatic reaction is for principals or the central office to provide additional remediation or install a new reading "program," what Morgan would consider evidence of "single-loop learning" and what Heifetz would call "technical solutions" (Heifetz & Linsky, 2002, p. 14).

What doesn't happen is encouraging real educational leadership (as opposed to management) through collaborative and considered attention to such questions as these:

- Are teachers being given the time they need to make sense of data and feedback *before* determining how to act?
- Who is doing the thinking that improved curriculum, teaching, and learning require? The central office? The state department of education? The principal? (The farther the thinking is from the classroom, the greater the likelihood of mechanistic teaching.)
- Does it make sense to teach reading as a distinct subject?
- Does students' proficiency at computer games suggest more effective ways to provide literacy instruction?
- Could something like interning in a hospital be more motivating for a student than having to pass a high-stakes exit exam?
- Are our limitations as administrators and teachers working in organizations bounded by convention and culture at the heart of the problem?

Addressing these types of questions requires that leaders create the conditions for "double-loop learning" and take on the adaptive work that developing innovative solutions requires. At Toyota, employees "have to operate in a culture where they constantly grapple with challenges and problems and must come up with fresh ideas" (Takeuchi, Osono, & Shimizu, 2008, p. 100). The corporation does not measure its success by quarterly earnings; rather its goals are "making people happy" and "delivering 'a full line in every market' to make employees feel they serve a useful purpose."

The deeper problem in school reform is that ultimately standards and targets are retrospective, not prospective. They build from the past, not the future. The standards inculcate current practice and do not take into consideration the role of teachers and school leaders as knowledge generators—those who will conduct the explorations and experiments on which improved practice will build. Standards encourage technical, short-term solutions rather than adaptive, long-term learning. They do not position school administrators (or those they supervise) as those who will lead inquiry. Standards encourage a stultified approach. Breaking free of this tendency toward stagnation is the challenge in teaching and coaching principals and other school leaders.

Present Conditions

In current policy and research, the school is considered to be the focal point for improving student achievement. A body of evidence from decades of school improvement efforts indicates that school leadership accounts for a significant part of improved performance (see, e.g., Bryk & Schneider, 2002). With the passage of the No Child Left Behind (NCLB) Act in 2001, the expectations for improved school performance and the necessity for improved leadership have increased.

For many additional reasons, ranging from changing demographics to improved technology, the complexity of the principal or director job has also increased. With the emphasis on improved student achievement at all levels of schooling, there is corresponding pressure for school leaders to be instructional leaders, and for school leaders to distribute leadership responsibilities within their school community (Spillane, 2006). And with the emergence of charter schools, EMOs, contracted services, online programs, and so forth, school leaders must increasingly be entrepreneurs (Hess, 2006).

At the same time, interest in school leadership positions on the part of prospective candidates has waned, partly because of their awareness of the increasing pressures and complexity of the job, and partly because compensation differentials with teachers have narrowed to the point that the incentives are not aligned with the expanded roles (Wallace Foundation, 2003).

Turnover in urban school and district leadership positions is high and consistent, averaging 15 percent annually in New York and other large cities. Yet research on leadership indicates that leadership stability and organizational performance are closely linked (Leithwood, Harris, & Hopkins, 2008). Widespread criticism of school leadership preparation programs has emerged, with concerns about applicant selection, as well as adequacy of training and internship experiences (Levin, 2006; Levine, 2005). At a global level, there is acknowledgment of a "talent shortage": the competition for increasingly competent leadership in every sector—corporate, government, nonprofit, religious—and the corresponding challenge of attracting performance-oriented leaders to the education sector (*Economist*, 2006).

The Typical Response

State governments and those conducting administrative training programs have responded to these conditions by developing:

- Standards for school leader preparation and evaluation (e.g., "Educational Leadership Policy Standards" [Council of Chief State School Officers, 2008])
- New state certification and licensure requirements
- Recertification requirements (after a specified number of years of service) for serving principals, superintendents, and other certificated administrators
- New evaluation instruments (e.g., School Leaders Licensure Assessment, Vanderbilt Assessment of Leadership in Education).
- Principal preparation programs attuned to the new standards and licensure requirements (e.g., University Council for Educational Administration, http://www.ucea.org)
- Alternative preparation programs that operate independent of the traditional university-based programs (e.g., New York City Leadership Academy; New Leaders for New Schools, Springfield, Massachusetts)
- Coaching and mentoring programs, both university- and district-based
- Bonus payment schemes for principals whose schools meet or exceed performance objectives (usually stated as test scores) (e.g., New York City Department of Education)

The problem with these responses is that the standards, certification programs, evaluation instruments, training programs, and incentive schemes tend to be normative, based on correlational research or expert judgment. But in the main they oversimplify the work of school leaders, failing to acknowledge many of the day-to-day duties and responsibilities and increasing complexities and expectations for school leaders. Such responses may make policy makers and academics feel better, but they have had little effect on changing the nature of the job, improving the candidate pool, increasing the quality of new appointees, or improving school performance.

What's Missing: Trust

Present policy on educational leadership standards (e.g., Educational Leadership Policy Standards [Council of Chief State School Officers, 2008]) makes instructional leadership the first priority, suggesting that school leaders need to devote the bulk of their time and attention to teaching and learning. Although it is hard to argue with a focus on instruction, I would contend that there is insufficient recognition in the current standards, evaluation instruments, and training program designs of the "fishbowl" dimension of school leadership—how the school leader is observed by every member of the school community, every minute of every day, and how the leader's moment-to-moment behavior is central to communicating mission, purpose, priorities, ethics, and so forth. That should be evident in the story of University City High School (see chapter 5).

Tony Bryk and Barbara Schneider's (2003) studies of school reform in Chicago provide particular insight into what they term "relational trust" as a precondition for school reform and improved school performance. In their view, "principals' actions play a key role in developing and sustaining relational trust" (p. 43). This trust is built through respectful exchanges with others, personal regard and commitment, competence in core role responsibilities, and personal integrity (pp. 41–44). Bryk and Schneider repeatedly emphasize, "As individuals interact with one another around the work of schooling, they are constantly discerning the intentions embedded in the actions of others" in regard to their own self-esteem and "their moral obligations to educate children well" (p. 41).

And it is through these interactions and the conduct of their duties and responsibilities that principals build the trust and confidence of teachers, students and their parents, and the community—without which change leadership, instructional improvement, program implementation, and process improvement cannot take place. For teachers, students, and parents, good management is assumed to be a prior condition for instructional leadership. And, for their part, true instructional leaders see the opportunity to teach in every encounter—whether a student discipline conference, a chance meeting with a teacher in the hallway, or a budget development session with the school management team.

The Centrality of Context and Related Factors

A significant shortcoming of current leadership standards and evaluation instruments is that they give almost no attention to context, including such obvious considerations as:

- The school or district history, financial well-being, human resources, employee relations, and prior leadership history
- Community characteristics, student body composition, political surroundings
- Curriculum, performance history, record-keeping and data systems, technology, facility design and conditions
- Governance structure and regulatory and policy coherence

In a recently published monograph, the National College for School Leadership (2007), England's foremost educational training and leadership development entity, puts it this way: "Successful leaders need to be 'contextually literate': they have to be able to 'read' their contexts like a text, including understanding the sub-texts, the meta-messages and the micropolitics whilst not becoming victims of them" (p. 5). For English academics and practitioners, the notion that "the environment in which a leader works strongly influences leadership" is the starting place for understanding "how leaders make a difference." In describing the entry processes I adopted as principal, regional superintendent, and superintendent, I have been trying to demonstrate that my success as a leader was heavily dependent on my ability to learn and interpret contextual factors and incorporate them in my leadership decisions.

A related consideration is succession planning and transition—the recruitment, entry, and support processes that are key factors in ensuring the appropriate match of candidate and position, and the role-shaping that determines how successfully the new appointee can go about creating the conditions for instructional leadership, a process that may take years (see Hart, 1993; Jentz, 2008). The ways in which districts, school boards (trustees), and school leadership councils manage these transitions have much to do with success in the principal or head position, and in a sense they are a part of the context one enters as a new leader. Such considerations are absent in evaluation protocols.

The conventions of school organization also constrain the possibilities for significant change. In discussing the relationship between our growing understanding of learning and teaching, and how they are influenced by school organization, Elmore concludes, "It is highly unlikely . . . that one could introduce the kinds of ideas suggested by the literature on best practice without upsetting the existing regularities of schooling" (1995, p. 372).

Time frame is another significant factor in evaluating leadership, especially given the accountability timetable of NCLB. If research suggests that a school turnaround takes three to five years, then a new school leader needs to be given three to five years to demon-strate improved performance. No matter how capable or innovative a new leader may be, he or she cannot reasonably be expected to build trust, improve school safety and working conditions, and improve test scores in the first year in the position.

Some aspects of school leadership are hard enough to define, let alone evaluate. For example, certain dimensions of the school leader or principal position are unique to the job—the speed of it, the number of interactions and decisions one engages in daily, its complexity, and the isolation and loneliness of it (see, e.g., Morris et al., 1984). Still other factors are important for leadership in any arena: self-knowledge (being in touch with one's passions, motivations, anxieties, competen-cies, and deficiencies), one's willingness to learn and to acknowledge what one does not know, and one's ability to truly listen and to empa-thize (see Goleman, 1997).

EXPANDING ROLES FOR SCHOOL LEADERS

Although there is little, if any, literature comparing the roles of public school principals, charter school directors, and parochial and inde-pendent school heads, the primary difference is that charter school directors and parochial and independent school heads are more like superintendents than principals. They report to a board of trustees and have complete responsibility for every aspect of their schools, from personnel to instruction to facilities. Not only must they lead and manage on a day-to-day basis, but they must also do long-range plan-ning, recruiting, marketing, and fund-raising.

The New York City Department of Education reform strategies initiated in 2007 assume that principals should have similar degrees of autonomy and accountability if their schools are going to make the quantum leaps in performance that the mayor and schools chancellor seek. Chicago, Boston, and Philadelphia are following similar strate-gies—more principal and school autonomy in exchange for increased accountability.

The increasingly complex and demanding responsibilities of the principalship in these cities and elsewhere raise two questions: Are principals adequately prepared to lead in these new conditions? And have the large urban districts developed sufficient organizational trust to encourage the risk-taking that autonomy and accountability require?

At present, there are few formal leadership development programs for those aspiring to these "new" positions, or support programs for those already in them. For the most part, school leaders must grow into the new responsibilities on their own or through networks they establish for themselves—they must learn on the job. To further complicate the task, the short-term time horizons mandated by NCLB (i.e., making adequate yearly progress) are not compatible with the time frames required to actually turn schools around. That situation is compounded when superintendents precipitously remove principals from their positions in the middle of the school year for alleged shortcomings or transgressions, as has frequently happened in Philadelphia over the past several years. Trust disappears and principals do as directed, not as professional judgment would warrant.[1]

Finally, given the range and complexity of factors related to leadership success and the increasing variety of school leadership positions, an additional question presents itself: Are the new standards, training programs, and evaluation instruments sufficient to ensure the success of school leaders?

A CRITIQUE OF CURRENT "SOLUTIONS"

In my view, there are at least three serious deficiencies in current thinking. The first is straightforward: When school leader performance is deemed inadequate by some criteria, what supports and interventions are available to improve leader performance? Where is one to learn the behaviors that characterize "effective" school leaders? The answers to these questions are starkly absent in the standards and evaluation policies and procedures states are putting forward. The belief seems to be that if various shortcomings are identified through whatever mechanism, then the leader will engage in self-improvement exercises leading to increased efficacy, a premise for which there is precious little support.

The second problem is obvious but still has not been not adequately addressed. Graduate programs in educational leadership, often linked to state certification requirements, presume that prospective school leaders can be taught most of what they need to know within twelve to twenty-four months of part-time study and a loosely supervised internship. Yet principals and superintendents routinely say that they learned 90 percent of what they needed to know to do

---

[1] Charter school directors may require principal certification, depending on state regulations, but parochial and independent school heads do not. In recognition of the challenges of school leadership, the National Association of Independent Schools is piloting a support program for newly appointed heads.

their jobs on the job. That suggests that school districts need to design continuous leadership development programs built into the ongoing work processes of the district because leadership learning and development are unending. But most districts make no serious commitment to leadership development, whether of teacher leaders, prospective administrators, or current administrators.

The third problem is more subtle and perhaps the most insidious: The seeds of failure are inherent in the current approaches to principal or school leader standards, licensure, evaluation instruments, and training programs. The conversation about instructional leadership has been and is being shaped by the NCLB Act, *Tough Choices or Tough Times* (National Center on Education and the Economy, 2007), and similar prescriptions for fixing American schools. The metrics of performance—test scores and school "report cards"—are based on cybernetic models that stipulate that improved performance requires that systems have the capacity to sense and monitor significant aspects of their environment, relate this information to the operating norms that guide system behavior, detect significant deviations from these norms, and initiate corrective action when discrepancies are detected (Morgan, 1997, p. 86). School improvement plans and corrective action plans thus assume a simple recursive model:

1. Review the evidence (descriptive and performance data).
2. Consider possible interventions (new curricula, organizational design, staffing, assessments, incentives, standards, etc.).
3. Implement these interventions.
4. Evaluate the outcomes.
5. Accumulate new evidence and return to step 1.

However, Schmoker reminds us that research on strategic planning indicates that "less than 10% of what gets planned actually gets implemented" because the exhaustive schedules of initiatives, action steps, and workshops are "only 'loosely-coupled' to the core process of teaching and its improvement" (2004, p. 427). Schmoker suggests, instead, that "the most productive thinking is continuous and simultaneous with action—that is, with teaching—as practitioners implement, assess, and adjust instruction as it happens."

Another shortcoming in most strategic planning exercises is that "many organizations have become proficient at single-loop learning, developing an ability to scan the environment, set objectives, and monitor the general performance of the system in relation to these objectives, . . . [keeping] the organization 'on course'" (Morgan, 1997,

p. 88). But, drawing on the work of Peter Senge and Donald Schoen, Morgan argues that

> To learn and change, organizational members must be skilled in understanding the assumptions, frameworks, and norms guiding current activity and be able to challenge and change them when necessary. . . . Organizational members must be skilled in understanding the paradigms, metaphors, mind-sets, or mental models that underpin how the organization operates . . . and develop new ones when appropriate. (1997, p. 88)

Conventional schools and conventional leadership are not going to generate the paradigm shifts that 100 percent proficiency (NCLB's 2014 goal) would require, or that would support the innovation and risk-taking that business and government leaders are calling for. As Senge argues:

> In a learning organization, leaders' roles differ dramatically from that of the charismatic decision maker. Leaders are designers, teachers, and stewards. These roles require new skills: the ability to build shared vision, to bring to the surface and challenge prevailing mental models, and to foster more systemic patterns of thinking. In short, leaders in learning organizations are responsible for building organizations where people are continually expanding their capabilities to shape the future—that is, leaders are responsible for learning. (1990, p. 9)

Senge also wonders whether the evolving demands of leadership, particularly in regard to "developing culture," will lead to a "new sort of management development [that] will focus on the roles, skills, and tools for leadership in learning organizations" (p. 22).

At the Wallace Foundation's fall 2007 conference on educational leadership, Rudy Crew, then CEO of the Miami-Dade public schools and formerly schools chancellor in New York City, and Joel Klein, current chancellor in New York, gave their answers to Senge's question. Crew spoke about how desperately he needed school leaders who were "learning to lead from the edge" and who didn't "fear the abyss." In his view, the dramatic differences in performance between urban and suburban students will only be removed when principals can "escape the tyranny of the day-to-day" and bring an entrepreneurial and innovative stance to their work.

Klein talked about the need for leaders "to be bolder" if such intractable problems as high school dropout rates are going to be resolved. Klein called for school leaders who see themselves as engaged in "changing the world." Crew and Klein agreed that talented leadership capable of addressing these challenges will only be attracted to the education sector if the conditions for creative intellectual work are in place. In their view, implementing the directives of others does not meet that standard. Nor do the current school leader evaluation instruments or school leadership standards.

A SOLUTION THAT CAN WORK: LEARNING TO LEAD AND LEADING FOR LEARNING

In conclusion, I will reiterate the pattern for approaching leadership roles that I first described in the Introduction. I have come to believe that this is an approach that can indeed work in addressing the central issues we are currently facing in educational reform:

- Take time to learn and read the context. Get to know the people, the place, the history, the formal and informal networks and power nodes, the conventions, and what matters to whom.
- Spend time in classrooms. That is where the real work of schooling takes place.
- Make sure basic operations continue to function while determining the work required to improve performance and the pace for doing it. Listen, watch, note, question, and take time to make sense of the data.
- In the design stage, first develop a thorough understanding of what went before, then decide what might be possible and where to go.
- Build—by developing human, social, organizational, and intellectual capital, and by reallocating resources (money, people, time, and space) to support the building.
- Be clear about purpose. Why are we doing this? To what end? Are students the beneficiaries of our work?
- Create an organizational culture that encourages and supports risk, inquiry, and entrepreneurship, and question convention and current practice.
- Rather than solve problems, set problems for others to solve.
- Monitor, track, and evaluate. Know what's improving and what needs attention. What is the evidence?
- Praise, honor, and celebrate accomplishments. Provide feedback.
- Take time to read, write, reflect, develop perspective, make sense, stay centered. Monitor yourself. Know yourself. Know what you're avoiding. (Finding time to do these things is much

easier if operational leadership responsibilities have been delegated to others.)

This list isn't meant to suggest a linear process; rather, all of the elements are recursive. I have tried to illustrate my evolution as leader in each chapter, using these precepts as a framework. I also recognize that with each change in position, I came to understand more and more clearly that the ways in which I went about learning the context had a great deal to do with building relational trust, and that without that trust I wasn't going to be able to move on to the next steps.

EVERYTHING TIES BACK TO THE CLASSROOM

As I read what I've written and listened to the stories I've told, I realize that there is a consistent pattern that is so obvious I've overlooked it. In every administrative position I've held, whether in schools or central office, I've always made time to be in classrooms, and not just to walk through. I needed to watch lessons unfold, see how students were responding, and have a relationship with teachers that allowed us to talk directly about the challenges and achievements of working with particular class groups or courses. I've needed to be close to classrooms and schools to have a sense of how student interests and culture change.

For me *leading for learning* has meant:

- Facilitating and enabling the creative energy in teaching teams.
- Regularly visiting classrooms and engaging teachers in conversations about teaching and learning.
- Resisting the pressure to solve problems, asking questions that move problem solving back to the place of the problem, setting the problem, and trusting that good solutions will emerge.
- At intervals (while I was in central office), assisting a third grade teacher in a nearby school or a fifth grade math teacher who was implementing a new math curriculum.
- Carefully observing classes, then, based on those observation, designing and conducting research and inquiry projects that addressed deep-seated assumptions and conventions about schooling.
- Recognizing that if teachers are expected to help every child, then every adult needs to be seen as capable of providing leadership in specific contexts and situations, and the entire faculty

and support staff need to work as a collective teaching and caring workforce.

- Considering meetings as opportunities to model engaging classroom practices.
- Creating opportunities for teachers and administrators to spend time in other schools and classrooms.
- Approaching teacher contract negotiations as an opportunity to focus on instructional improvement, rather than on wages, benefits, and working conditions.
- Making data public and considering it as communal property; using data as the starting place for inquiry.

By continually taking time to learn what teachers or principals were planning and thinking about, I've been able to respond to their interests and concerns.

By taking time to learn about the "hidden" competencies and interests of support staff, teachers, and administrators, I've been able to help them put their abilities into the service of students in ways that energized them and their students.

In seeing myself as "lead teacher" in every administrative position I've held, I've been careful and intentional about designing meetings, providing articles and books to read, and suggesting resources that model highly engaging teaching and learning.

As lead learner, I have made it a practice to join leadership development or teacher training programs as a participant.

As a "reflective practitioner," I've made it a part of my practice to write, research, and publish about my work, whether locally or nationally, and to take an inquiry stance on problems, challenges, and opportunities.

As a "resource manager," I have always made sure that the schools or districts I've lead have enough discretionary funding and enough time (for professional development; books, materials, supplies and equipment; travel; consulting help) so that I could always say "Yes" when teachers and staff members came forward with ideas they wanted to pursue.

Because my entire administrative career has been in urban schools, I have been intentional about identifying community resources that could enhance opportunities to learn for students and employees.

In every leadership position I've held, whether in schools or central office, I've created supportive, professional work environments, which have attracted excellent teachers and administrators motivated by professional commitment. Supporting them has been the key to the successes I have had.

My approach has always been to value and respect local knowledge; to take time to learn who, what, and where; and to consider local knowledge as the most accessible intellectual and social capital.

In every organization I have led, student achievement and performance on a range of indicators have improved in ways that mattered to a cross-section of stakeholders—the state, the school board, my superordinates, colleagues, the employees I supervised, parents, and students themselves. I'd like to think that those successes demonstrate that district, school, and student performance can improve without coercive policies and practices.

My hope is that in telling these stories and making these arguments, I have made some small contribution to our collective understanding of what it means to lead for learning, and of how one learns to lead.

Bibliography

Artiles, A. J., Klinger, J. K., & Tate, W. F. (Eds.). (2006, August/September). Theme Issue: Representation of minority students in special education: Complicating traditional explanations. *Educational Researcher, 35*(6).

Bello. (1995). High school is a sea of chaos. *Philadelphia Daily News*, 3.

Bennis, W. (1989). *Why leaders can't lead: The unconscious conspiracy continues.* San Francisco: Jossey-Bass.

Block, P. (1997, Winter). The end of leadership. *Leader to Leader*, 11–14.

Bryk, A. S., & Schneider, B. (2002). *Trust in schools: A core resource for improvement.* New York: Sage.

Bryk, A. S., & Schneider, B. (2003, March). Trust in schools: A core resource for school reform. *Educational Leadership*, 40–44.

Cambron-McCabe, N., Cunningham, L., Harvey, J., & Koff, R. (2005). *The superintendent's fieldbook: A guide for leaders of learning.* Thousand Oaks, CA: Corwin.

Christensen, C. M., Horn, M. B., & Johnson, C. W. (2008). *Disrupting class: How disruptive innovation will change the way the world learns.* New York: McGraw-Hill.

Christensen, C. M., & Overdorf, M. (2000, March–April). Meeting the challenge of disruptive change. *Harvard Business Review*, 67–74.

Cochran-Smith, M., & Lytle, S. L. (2009). *Inquiry as stance: Practitioner research in the next generation.* New York: Teachers College Press.

Collins, J. (2001). *Good to great.* New York: HarperCollins.

Collins, J. (2005). *Good to great and the social sectors: A monograph to accompany Good to Great.* Boulder, CO: Jim Collins.

Copland, M. A. (2003). Leadership of inquiry: Building and sustaining capacity for school improvement. *Educational Evaluation and Policy Analysis, 25*(4), 375–395.

Council of Chief State School Officers (CCSSO). (1996). *Interstate School Leaders Licensure Consortium: Standards for school leaders.* Washington, DC: CCSSO.

Council of Chief State School Officers (CCSSO). (2008). *Educational leadership policy standards: ISLLC 2008*. Washington, DC: CCSSO.

David, J. L. (2008, March). What research says about grade retention. *Educational Leadership*, 84–85.

Dawson, L. J., & Quinn, R. (2004, November). Coherent governance. *The School Administrator*, 29–32.

De Geus, A. P. (1988, March–April). Planning as learning. *Harvard Business Review*, 70–74.

DePree, M. (1989). *Leadership is an art*. New York: Dell.

Donaldson, G. A. (2001). *Cultivating leadership in schools: Connecting people, purpose, and practice*. New York: Teachers College.

Economist. (2006, October 7). The talent shortage [theme issue].

Elmore, R. F. (1995, August). Teaching, learning, and school organization: Principles of practice and the regularities of schooling. *Educational Administration Quarterly, 31*(3), 355–374.

Elmore, R. F. (2000, Winter). Building a new structure for leadership. Washington, DC: The Albert Shanker Institute.

Erickson, F. (1987, November). Conceptions of school culture: An overview. *Educational Administration Quarterly, 23*(4), 11–24.

Evans, R. (1996). *The human side of school change: Reform, resistance, and the real-life problems of innovation*. San Francisco: Jossey-Bass.

Fullan, M. (1993). *Change forces: Probing the depths of educational reform*. London: Falmer.

Fullan, M. (1999). *Change forces: The sequel*. Philadelphia: Falmer.

Fullan, M. (2001). *Leading in a culture of change*. San Francisco: Jossey-Bass.

Fullan, M., Hill, P., & Crevola, C. (2006). *Breakthrough*. Thousand Oaks, CA: Corwin.

Gardner, H. (1995). *Leading minds: An anatomy of leadership*. New York: Basic Books.

Goffee, R., & Jones, G. (2000, September–October). Why should anyone be led by you? *Harvard Business Review*, 63–70.

Goleman, D. (1997). *Emotional intelligence: Why it can matter more than IQ*. New York: Bantam Books.

Goodlad, John I. (1984). *A place called school: Prospects for the future*. New York: McGraw-Hill.

Hargreaves, A., & Fink, D. (2006). *Sustainable leadership*. San Francisco: Jossey-Bass.

Hargreaves, D. H. (1997). A road to the learning society. *School Leadership and Management, 17*(1), 9–21.

Hargreaves, D. H. (2003a, January). *From improvement to transformation*. Lecture presented at the International Congress for School Effectiveness and Improvement, Sydney, Australia. Available at http://www.icsei.net/fileadmin/ICSEI/user_upload/documents/David_Hargreaves_ICSEI_keynote_2003_-_From_improvement_to_transformation.pdf.

Hargreaves, D. H. (2003b, May). *Leadership for transformation within the London Challenge*. London, UK: Annual Lecture of the London Leadership Centre.

Hart, A. W. (1993). *Principal succession: Establishing leadership in schools.* Albany: State University of New York.

Heifetz, R. A. (1994). *Leadership without easy answers.* Cambridge, MA: Belknap Harvard.

Heifetz, R. A., & Linsky, M. (2002). *Leadership on the line: Staying alive through the dangers of leading.* Cambridge, MA: Harvard Business School.

Hess, F. M. (2006). *Education entrepreneurship: Realities, challenges, possibilities.* Cambridge, MA: Harvard.

Hess, F. M. (Ed.). (2008). *The future of education entrepreneurship: Possibilities for school reform.* Cambridge, MA: Harvard.

Hong, H., & Yu, B. (2007, December). Early-grade retention and children's reading and math learning in elementary years. *Educational Evaluation and Policy Analysis, 29*(4), 239–261.

Jentz, B. (with Wofford, J.). (2008). *The EntryPlan approach: How to begin a leadership position successfully* (education edition). Newton, MA: Leadership and Learning, Inc. Available at http://www.entrybook.com.

Jentz, B. C., & Murphy, J. T. (2005a, January). Embracing confusion: What leaders do when they don't know what to do. *Phi Delta Kappan, 86*(5), 358–366.

Jentz, B. C., & Murphy, J. T. (2005b, June). Starting confused: How leaders start when they don't know where to start. *Phi Delta Kappan, 86*(10), 736–744.

Johnson, S. M. (1996). *Leading to change: The challenge of the new superintendency.* San Francisco: Jossey-Bass.

Kegan, R., & Lahey, L. L. (2001). *How the way we talk can change the way we work: Seven languages for transformation.* San Francisco: Jossey-Bass.

Leithwood, K., Harris, A., & Hopkins, D. (2008, February). Seven strong claims about successful school leadership. *School Leadership and Management, 28*(1), 27–42.

Leithwood, K., Jantzi, D., & Steinbach, R. (1999). *Changing leadership for changing times.* Philadelphia: Open University Press.

Levin, H. M. (2006, November). Can research improve educational leadership? *Educational Researcher,* 38–43.

Levine, A. (2005, March). *Educating school leaders.* Washington, DC: The Educating Schools Project (www.edschools.org).

Lortie, D. C. (1975). *Schoolteacher: A sociological study.* Chicago: University of Chicago Press.

Lytle, J. H. (1980, June). An untimely (but significant) experiment in teacher motivation. *Phi Delta Kappan, 61*(10), 700–702.

Lytle, J. H. (1988, February). Is special education serving minority students? *Harvard Educational Review, 58*(1), 116–123.

Lytle, J. H. (1996, June). The inquiring manager: Developing new structures to support reform. *Phi Delta Kappan, 77,* 664–670.

Lytle, J. H. (1998, April). *Using chaos theory to inform high school redirection.* Paper presented at the American Educational Research Association Annual Meeting, San Diego, CA.

Lytle, J. H. (2002, October). Whole school reform from the inside. *Phi Delta Kappan, 84*(2), 164–167.

Lytle, J. H. (2004, November). Heifetz and the notion of "I, Superintendent." *The School Administrator, 61*(10), 24–25.

Lytle, J. H. (2009, May). The context of superintendent entry. *The School Administrator,* 10–15.

March, J. G. (1978, February). American public school administration: A short analysis. *School Review,* 217–250.

Marzano, R. J., Waters, T., & McNulty, B. A. (2005). *School leadership that works: From research to results.* Alexandria, VA, and Aurora, CO: ASCD & Mid-Continent Research for Education and Learning.

Morgan, G. (1997). *Images of organization* (2nd ed.). Thousand Oaks, CA: Sage.

Morris, V. C., Crowson, R. L., Porter-Gehrie, C., & Hurwitz, E., Jr. (1984). *Principals in action: The reality of managing schools.* Columbus, OH: Merrill.

Murphy, J. (Ed.). (2002). *The educational leadership challenge: Redefining leadership for the 21st century.* Chicago: National Society for the Study of Education at the University of Chicago.

Murphy, J. (2005). *Connecting teacher leadership and school improvement.* Thousand Oaks, CA: Corwin.

Murphy, J. (2006). *Preparing school leaders: Defining a research and action agenda.* Lanham, MD: Rowman & Littlefield.

Murphy, J., & Datnow, A. (Eds.). (2003). *Leadership lessons from comprehensive school reform.* Thousand Oaks, CA: Corwin.

Murphy, J., & Louis, K. S. (1999). *Handbook of research on educational administration: A project of the American Educational Research Association* (2nd ed.). San Francisco: Jossey-Bass.

National Center on Education and the Economy. (2007). *Tough choices or tough times: The report of the New Commission on the Skills of the American Workforce.* San Francisco: Jossey-Bass.

National College for School Leadership (NCSL). (2007, May). *What we know about school leadership.* Available at http://www.nationalcollege.org.uk/publications.

Sanaghan, P., & Lytle, J. H. (2008, January). Creating a transition map for a new superintendency: 7 powerful strategies. *AASA New Superintendents E-Journal.* Available at http://www.aasa.org/publications/content.cfm?Item Number=9646.

Schmoker, M. (1999). *Results: The key to continuous improvement.* Alexandria, VA: ASCD.

Schmoker, M. (2004, February). Tipping point: From feckless reform to substantive instructional improvement. *Phi Delta Kappan,* 424–433.

Schon, D. A. (1983). *The reflective practitioner: How professionals think in action.* New York: Basic Books.

Seligman, M. (1975). *Helplessness: On depression, development, and death.* San Francisco: W. H. Freeman.

Senge, P. M. (1990). *The fifth discipline: The art & practice of the learning organization.* New York: Doubleday.

Senge, P. M. (1990, Fall). The leader's new work: Building learning organizations. *Sloan Management Review,* 7–23.

Sparks, D. (2005). *Leading for results: Transforming teaching, learning, and relationships in schools.* Thousand Oaks, CA: Corwin.

Spillane, J. P. (2006). *Distributed leadership.* San Francisco: Jossey-Bass.

Stein, S. J., & Gwirtzman, L. (2003). *Principal training on the ground: Ensuring highly qualified leadership.* Portsmouth, NH: Heinemann.

Takeuchi, H., Osono, E., & Shimizu, N. (2008, June). The contradictions that drive Toyota's success. *Harvard Business Review,* 96–104.

Tichy, N. M. (with Cardwell, N.). (2002). *The cycle of leadership: How great leaders teach their companies to win.* New York: HarperCollins.

Trenton Times. (1998, August 28). Editorial: The "fishbowl" strategy, 10.

Wagner, T. (1998, March). Change as collaborative inquiry: A "constructivist" methodology for reinventing schools. *Phi Delta Kappan,* 512–517.

Wagner, T., Kegan, R., Lahey, L., Lemons, R. W., Garnier, J., Helsing, D., et al. (2006). *Change leadership: A practical guide to transforming our schools.* San Francisco: Jossey-Bass.

Wallace Foundation. (2003). *Beyond the pipeline: Getting the principals we need, where they are needed most.* New York: The Wallace Foundation.

Weick, K. E., & Sutcliffe, K. M. (2001). *Managing the unexpected: Assuring high performance in an age of complexity.* San Francisco: Jossey-Bass.

Wetlaufer, S. (1999, March–April). Driving change: An interview with Ford Motor Company's Jacques Nasser. *Harvard Business Review,* 77–88.

Wheatley, M. J. (1992). *Leadership and the new science: Learning about organization from an orderly universe.* San Francisco: Barrett-Koehler.

Yoffie, D. B., & Cusumano, M. A. (1999, January–February). Judo strategy: The competitive dynamics of Internet time. *Harvard Business Review,* 71–81.

USEFUL WEBSITES

Center for Creative Leadership — http://www.ccl.org

Center for Public Leadership, Kennedy School of Government, Harvard University — http://content.ksg.harvard.edu/leadership

Center on Reinventing Public Education, University of Washington — http://www.crpe.org

Center for the Study of Teaching and Policy, University of Washington — http://depts.washington.edu/ctpmail

Schools of Education and related centers at Harvard, Vanderbilt, Stanford, and University of Virginia

State and district sites — Easily found through an Internet search engine

University Council for Educational Administration — http://www.ucea.org

Wallace Foundation — http://www.wallacefoundation.org

JOURNALS DESERVING OF REGULAR PERUSAL

Administrative Science Quarterly
American School Board Journal
Chronicle of Higher Education
Educational Leadership (ASCD)
Educational Administration Quarterly
Educational Evaluation and Policy Analysis (AERA)
Education Week
Harvard Business Review (in particular, the special issues on leadership: December 2001, January 2004, and January 2007)
Independent School (for the private school perspective)
NASSP Bulletin and *NAEP Bulletin* (for a sense of what principals are thinking)
Phi Delta Kappan
School Administrator (for a sense of what superintendents are thinking)

About the Author

James H. (Torch) Lytle, Ed.D., is currently practice professor of educational leadership at the Graduate School of Education, University of Pennsylvania. From 1998 to 2006, Lytle was superintendent of the Trenton, New Jersey, public schools, where he led an aggressive effort to implement New Jersey's urban education reform initiative. Prior to his appointment in Trenton, he served in a variety of capacities in the school district of Philadelphia as an elementary, middle, and high school principal; executive director for planning, research, and evaluation; regional superintendent; and assistant superintendent.

Lytle has been active in a number of national professional organizations, including the Council of Great City Schools, the Cross Cities Campaign, and the American Educational Research Association. He has written and presented frequently on matters relating to the improvement of urban schooling. His teaching and research interests relate to increasing the efficacy of urban public schools, managing leadership transitions, and leading school change efforts. He has been a consultant to the Wallace/Reader's Digest Foundation and Council of Chief State School Officers project on school leadership development.

Lytle received his doctorate in education from Stanford, his master's degree in English from the State University of New York at Buffalo, and his bachelor's degree from Cornell University.